Praise for
I AM REDEEMED

"Knowing Mike nearly from the time both of our groups started, I've only seen his heart for the Lord grow stronger. His transparency and depth speak with love. I encourage you to read what Mike has to share in *I Am Redeemed*."

BART MILLARD | MercyMe

"Like Mike's chart-topping proclamation in the song 'Redeemed,' his road-to-redemption story through great personal challenge is equally inspirational. The music of Big Daddy Weave continues to impact countless lives—and you'll better understand why after you read Jim Scherer's riveting account of Mike's journey from self-loathing and questioning God to the liberating realization that we are all children of the King no matter what."

MATT CROUCH | President and Chairman,
Trinity Broadcasting Network

Mike has always welcomed me with the greatest warmth, kindness, and humor. This book does the same. It is life giving.

LUKE SMALLBONE | for KING & COUNTRY

"As with their music, the story that Mike Weaver shares in *I Am Redeemed* is one of grace, love, and redemption. As you read this book, I believe you will come away with a fresh and inspired view of how much the Father loves you and how His plans never fail. It's an honor to know Mike and to have shared in some of the moments in the journey of Big Daddy Weave over the years. Their partnership with K-LOVE is a special one indeed, and for that we are fortunate and thankful."

DAVID PIERCE | Chief of Ministry Partnerships,
K-LOVE and Air1

"Betty and I love to hear Big Daddy Weave sing 'Redeemed.' It thrills the hearts of everyone, everywhere. Mike Weaver, the cowriter of that song, told me that when he was a boy, his dad was greatly impacted by my messages and our television broadcast. To God be the glory! Since then, God has used Mike's testimony to inspire and encourage people around the world. I believe his journey, which Mike shares with vulnerability in these pages, will help readers find freedom from their past failures—and point them to our Great Redeemer."

JAMES ROBISON | Founder and President,
LIFE Outreach International, Fort Worth, Texas

"Since first touring with Mike sixteen years ago, I've been honored to see the way he loves everyone he comes in contact with. Through *I Am Redeemed*, he is able to share his story and the journey of the powerful song 'Redeemed.' And all the while he points to the grace and love of Jesus in a way that only Mike Weaver can. Way to go my friend!"

REBECCA ST. JAMES | GRAMMY® Award–Winning
Singer/Songwriter

"I've always known Mike Weaver as a prolific singer. How refreshing to see that he is just as anointed as an author. I'm thankful for the way that he led me in worship through the pages of this book."

DAVID NASSER | Senior VP of Spiritual Development,
Liberty University

"This book is a faithful reminder that even in our darkest days, God is still with us, helping us with the struggles that we may not understand in the moment. If we trust in Him during these challenges, His plans are always better than ours."

ZACH WILLIAMS | GRAMMY® Award–Winning
Singer/Songwriter

"To the military veterans that Operation Restored Warrior (ORW) has the honor to work with, I often say, 'The glory of your life is in direct proportion to the assault set against it!' That statement could not be truer for Mike and Jay Weaver. Through all that has been set against the Weaver brothers, the gift of their life-changing songs has been birthed. The world is a better place because of Big Daddy Weave and their music. If you read one book this year, make it *I Am Redeemed*. You will laugh and cry through it all, and you will be blessed and embraced by the loving grace of Jesus."

PAUL LAVELLE | CMSgt, USAF, (Ret), MSC, and
Founder of Operation Restored Warrior

"*I Am Redeemed* is Mike Weaver's beautiful and moving testimony to his lifelong walk with Jesus. We at World Vision are grateful for the thousands of lives he and his Big Daddy Weave bandmates have touched, sparking transformation not just for the children who are sponsored but also for the concertgoers who hear about God's love for the poor. Mike honestly shares the ups and downs in his life, pointing to Jesus, who is ever faithful and has redeemed us and made us a 'new creation' (2 Corinthians 5:17)."

EDGAR SANDOVAL SR. | President of World Vision U.S.

"In *I Am Redeemed*, we get a raw perspective from Mike Weaver, a man God uses to influence the world through his work with Big Daddy Weave. It is so refreshing to see his transparent, unfiltered journey of the internal struggles we all face and how God has redeemed them. It encourages me to know that if Mike came through those struggles praising God, so can I. This book will inspire you to press into the power and understanding of our precious Jesus."

AUTUMN MILES | CEO Autumn Miles Ministries,
Host Autumn Miles Show, Author of *Appointed*,
I am Rahab, and *Gangster Prayer*

I Am REDEEMED

LEARNING TO LIVE IN GRACE

MIKE WEAVER

AND JIM SCHERER

WORTHY®
PUBLISHING

New York • Nashville

Worthy
Hachette Book Group
1290 Avenue of the Americas, New York, NY 10104

worthypublishing.com
twitter.com/worthypub
First Edition: September 2019
Worthy is a division of Hachette Book Group, Inc. The Worthy name and logo are trademarks of Hachette Book Group, Inc.

The publisher is not responsible for websites (or their content) that are not owned by the publisher.

Cover photo by David Molnar.
Cover design by Edward Crawford.
Print book interior design by Bart Dawson.

Cataloging-in-Publication Data is on file with the Library of Congress.

ISBNs: 978-1-5460-3358-5 (hardcover), 978-1-5491-8354-6 (downloadable audio), 978-1-5460-1499-7 (ebook)

Printed in the United States of America
LSC-C
10 9 8 7 6 5 4 3 2

For my dad, Russ Weaver.

This book is dedicated to:
Kandice,
Eli,
Zeke,
Naomi,
my mother, Pat,
Jay,
Emily,
Makenzie,
Maddie,
Nathan,
and all of my family.

CONTENTS

PREFACE

Like most ideas Mike shares with me, the thought for this book was born out of the faithfulness in Mike's heart. Mike's redeemed experience, which you'll read about in the pages ahead, led to his writing the song "Redeemed." Ever since "Redeemed" was released, stories have poured in from people who have had similar life-changing experiences.

Mike came to me saying that we should share in a book what happened to him and what we've learned through his experiences that could help others. At the same time, it was important to him that we be transparent about the struggles that still occur in his life and what he's learning along the way.

We began writing this book together and at one point thought it was complete. Then, in 2017, things we never would have imagined began happening. The depth and weight of those events put the book on hold for well over a year while all of us grappled with the situations at hand. Later, when we began to put those events on paper, we realized how much more we had been shown that could help others.

That is how we came to the book you have today. Through it, Mike and I want you to know that you are not alone. The struggles you face are not yours to battle by yourself. Even more so, we want you to know there is life and life in abundance for you. Our deepest desire is that in reading these words, you will find, embrace, and live in the identity offered to you in the gift of grace.

—Jim Scherer

INTRODUCTION

For much of my life, my perception of myself was dogged by lies that worked their way into my heart. Those lies told me I was something to be hated. I loathed myself. One day God spoke into me with a revelation that changed everything. I shared that word through writing the song "Redeemed," recorded by our group Big Daddy Weave. Thousands of people told us how this good news dramatically changed their lives. Many who had also dealt with the liar who tried to devour me were now seeing God's redemption doing amazing things in their lives.

It would be great if that were the end of the story. In truth, since that day when I heard God tell me how much He loved me, I've been pulled many times into that old self that can't see me the way God sees me. I've often struggled to live in the peace He purchased for me, even to the point of arguing with God that He must be wrong about me.

Thankfully, God continued teaching me and still is all the time. In this book I will share the revelations learned in my journey that have brought me closer to the life God intends for all of us. Through these words, Jim and I pray that God leads you to a deep, intimate understanding of His love for you, that He will reveal how precious you are to Him, that you will grow in the identity purchased for you, and that you will go forward in the peace of being redeemed.

—Mike Weaver

1

THE GREAT LIAR

Storms had threatened all day, but beams of afternoon sun began to break through the clouds as our car pulled up on 5th Avenue in downtown Nashville, Tennessee. We stepped out of the car and onto a bright red carpet that stretched nearly a city block along the outside of the Ryman Auditorium to the historic music venue's entrance. Hundreds of music fans cheered and waved while camera crews and press stopped us for interviews as we made our way into the first-ever K-LOVE Fan Awards.

As honored as the other guys in Big Daddy Weave and I were to be there, the red carpet was a source of anxiety for me from the moment I heard about it. I've always hated certain aspects of these

3

kinds of events. Those negative feelings are primarily rooted in my own insecurities. The way I've seen myself and have perceived other people seeing me over the years was the beginning of the very song that brought us here.

I was blown away when I first heard we were even nominated for an award, let alone for Song of the Year. Making it even more meaningful was that the winners would be decided by radio listener votes. Most other awards are decided by committees or industry members. This was an event for the people. Every one of those votes represented a life that had been touched in some way by the message in the music.

In my mind we had no chance of winning. I wasn't bothered by that because I'm such a big fan of everyone else who was nominated. There was no way an award was going to us instead of artists like Chris Tomlin or Matt Redman, people we respect and looked forward to being in the same room with that night.

I was so sure we wouldn't win that I didn't even have a speech prepared. My six-year-old son, Eli, said to me earlier that night, "Daddy, I'm nervous. What will happen if you don't win?" I told him not to worry. We had already won knowing how God had used the song in so many people's lives.

We made our way into the Ryman Auditorium and found the pews where we were to sit. The Ryman was originally built as a house of worship in the late 1800s. I felt more like I was in church than at an awards show, except that I was surrounded by my favorite Christian music artists. It was surreal. I loved being there with my wife,

Kandice, and the other Big Daddy Weave guys and their wives. For as much time as the five of us in Big Daddy Weave had spent together, there had been only a few times when we and the very special women in our lives had been together.

When the time approached for us to perform our nominated song, we left our seats to walk backstage. On the way, we passed by Toby-Mac. As we did, I thought about how I'd listened to TobyMac and dc Talk since I was a teenager. I couldn't believe we were here among all these people who have had such an impact on my life.

Standing side stage about to go on, I thought about the people who had stood on this very spot—Hank Williams, Elvis Presley, and so many others. In just a moment we were going to stand in that same place and sing of what Jesus had done in our lives.

The time came for us to play. I don't consider us in the same league as the people I was seeing in the audience during our performance, like Mac Powell from Third Day and Bart Millard from MercyMe. It moved me to be singing a song in front of them that meant so much to my life. Seeing the looks on their faces, seeing that they were receiving what we were sharing, is a moment I'll never forget.

Back in our seats, the time came for the announcement of the Song of the Year award. Suddenly my heart started beating faster. "Redeemed" being voted Song of the Year wasn't something I'd even considered possible, but I could feel the anxiousness increasing in my mind and body. What if they *did* say our name? What would I say?

Then Mandisa read, "The Song of the Year is . . . 'Redeemed'! Big Daddy Weave!" When I heard those words, my mind left me, and my body went into autopilot mode. Our friend Chris August was jumping up and down in front of us. I didn't even remember that my wife was there. I just left the pew and thought, *I need to get to that podium before anyone else so I can figure out what I can possibly say. Can we even respond to what is happening? How in the world am I going to process this?* I could only think about Eli feeling nervous and the news I could tell him when we got home.

I didn't know exactly what I was saying at the time. I only knew that I was speaking words of gratitude. I was so grateful for the opportunity to thank God in front of everybody. I had set myself up not to care about being nominated for an award, let alone actually receiving one. I really thought it didn't affect me, but it was a wonderful feeling. It's not like I thought we deserved it, but it was awesome that it happened.

This experience that all started with a song that came together in my bedroom turned even more surreal. We left the podium and entered the side stage area, where the first people to congratulate us were the show's hosts—Phil, Miss Kay, and Jase Robertson from our favorite TV show, *Duck Dynasty*. They were giving us props and patting us on the back. I was sure I was about to wake up any second from some weird *Duck Dynasty* dream.

As sweet and special as all of that was, we still knew what we had won in the journey leading up to this point was the most important thing of all. The icing on the cake was being able to talk about what the Lord had done in my life and the lives of others.

When the Lord moves in your life in a real and personal way, no one can ever take it away from you. People can try, but there's something ironclad about having an experience with the very real God. It's like what the Lord said to the people of Israel, "My Presence will go with you" (Exodus 33:14). After that, a beautiful thing happens when you share your experience with others. They become hungry for their own personal encounter with Him.

A week after the awards show, still in the afterglow of all that happened, I played an event without the other Big Daddy Weave guys at a youth camp. My family was with me, and we were having a great time. Not long after we had been there, I began to wake up at night thinking how stupid I must have sounded giving the acceptance speech at the K-LOVE Fan Awards.

Part of celebrating the recognition of "Redeemed" was celebrating the victory in my life over self-hatred, not feeling good enough, and reliving things over and over in my mind that I was disappointed about in myself. Now all of that was happening again. It was the most disheartening feeling. To be back at square one just one week later was one of the most hopeless feelings in my life. I didn't know how I could ever get up in front of anybody again.

I didn't realize it then, but I was listening to the voice of the great liar. The enemy's long-term, unchanging strategy is to tell us lie after lie about ourselves. The apostle John wrote, "When [Satan] lies, he speaks his native language, for he is a liar and the father of lies" (John 8:44). Sadly, we're often all too eager to listen.

The enemy was speaking a small falsehood into my mind where he knew I was the weakest. I added all the other ingredients to make it grow into something overwhelming. I was angry, scared, and all the other things the enemy hoped I would be. Perhaps most ironic of all, I felt powerless.

Isn't that exactly what you would expect the enemy of the Lord to want us to feel? Here I was, having experienced an encounter with the almighty Lord of the universe who clothes me in righteousness, turning my back to that truth to embrace hate for myself because I "might" have said something that sounded stupid. It sounds insane, but perhaps you've experienced these lies as well and know exactly what I'm talking about.

Thanks to those lies and me believing them, I hated myself for most of my life. My perception of myself was like someone whose house is filled with those fun house mirrors that distort what you look like. When I looked at myself, I hated the way I looked, hated what I said, hated what I did, and hated who I was. I did that because I was looking into a mirror created and held to my face by the deceiver. Then one day, thanks be to God, I saw myself in the mirror of grace. Even though I had known the Lord and had loved Him, I had never looked at myself the way He does—covered in His love, redeemed by His sacrifice.

God means for you and me to see ourselves in the mirror of His grace. Some get there right away while others battle trying to see it, as I did for many years, beginning when I was just a small boy.

2

THE ROOTS
OF IDENTITY

The roots of identity begin in our earliest days of childhood. My family moved to Gulf Breeze, Florida, from Michigan when I was four years old. We lived two blocks north of a body of water we can now see from my parents' house called the Santa Rosa Sound. The Sound and a thin strip of land south of it were all that separated our house from the Gulf of Mexico.

My dad worked in civil service. He was able to apply for a transfer to Florida because of the level of his GS, or General Service, number. Even as a child, I was aware of that GS number. The higher the number, the better the work opportunities. Dad was offered a job at the Pensacola Naval Air Station working in computers back in the old mainframe days.

As a kid, I never exactly fit in. Not long after we moved to Gulf Breeze, I entered the first kindergarten class of the brand-new Oriole Beach Elementary School, not far from my house. My mom recalls a day when I came home and said I didn't want to go to school anymore. She didn't know what had happened, and whatever it was is blocked in my memory, but I never wanted to ride the school bus again. All I can remember are the unfriendly faces of older kids on the bus and the playground and being afraid.

Other events related to school also shaped how I felt about myself. One of those times was when my first-grade teacher told us that writing a lowercase letter *e* was kind of like drawing a Pac-Man. Pac-Man was an arcade game that was really big at that time. Sometime later, she asked if anyone could draw a Pac-Man. I went up to the board and wrote the letter *e*, because I was going to impress her that I remembered what she had said. Everybody laughed because, of course, that's not what a Pac-Man really looks like. I felt so stupid, so let down. I wanted to leave. I never volunteered for anything again. It sounds like a stupid thing, but it affected me deeply and stayed with me even into my adult years.

There were some things I did love about school. I loved when the teacher would change the room to fit a different season. I enjoyed the stories teachers would read to us. Stories were always meaningful for me. We also had something similar to music appreciation that I loved where we got to play recorders and make music with drums and sticks. We eventually got to where we could perform the melody of "That's What Friends Are For" on our recorders, which was a big deal for us fourth graders.

I wanted to love physical education. I thought some of the things they were doing were cool, but I always stunk at everything in PE. It was another one of those places where I never felt good enough. I either couldn't keep up, wasn't as fast as other kids, or wasn't as strong as other children.

We had a teacher at Oriole Beach Elementary School named Miss Ramsey. In the third grade we had to do little dances, act out scenes, and put on plays. One day we had to do the Mexican hat dance. Nobody ever picked me to be their dance partner, so I ended up having to dance with Miss Ramsey. Miss Ramsey was a large-chested woman, and I was the height of an average third grader. The two of us dancing closely together nearly gave me a concussion from the repeated beating occurring on top of my head!

Aside from being my dance partner, Miss Ramsey noticed my voice. She chose me to perform the lead role of Scarecrow Rick in a fifth-grade play, which was a big deal. At another time Miss Ramsey had me make an appearance as Frosty the Snowman in a perfectly round Frosty costume. It was the beginning of a spark in me for music.

Those introductions to the power of music were the brighter side of my education experience. The darker side of school was dealing with the kids who looked down on me. These kids were always picking on somebody, always doing little things to get under people's skin.

A particularly dark day in the sixth grade was when one of those kids tripped me as I was getting off the school bus. I went headfirst down the bus steps and received such a severe concussion that I had temporary amnesia.

Outside of school, I played with the kids in my neighborhood. I wanted them to like me so much that I would give them my things, even gifts I had just received for my birthday. I wanted to feel like we were on the same team; I wanted them to feel about me like I felt about them.

I made a few friends, but home was my haven. Home was where I felt safe with my mom and dad. My little brother, Jay, and I were buds from day one and always played together. I have such fond memories of growing up with him. We became even greater friends as we grew together into our middle school years. Even when he was very small, he was kind of a hero to me. I always thought he was the greatest.

When I was in the sixth grade, kids in my neighborhood came over to our house. They weren't my friends, but they would randomly show up when they were bored. I was so desperate for them to like me that I would do whatever they wanted to do. On this day they wanted to wrestle. They were all ganging up on me, holding me down. They weren't doing it in a mean way, just playing around. All of a sudden Jay came flying over the azalea bushes. Jay, a little third grader, then proceeded to whoop those three sixth graders! Like I said, he was my hero.

Much later, as the Lord was doing a big work in my life when I was in my twenties, I asked my dad about my childhood experiences.

Why would something people said when I was small or something that happened when I was little still affect me so much as a grown man? My dad told me that if those same events happened to me now, it wouldn't affect me as much because I've formed an identity of who I am as a man. Since it happened when I was a small child, it was at a time when the foundation of my identity was being formed. Those negative experiences with my peers occurred at a time when I had not yet accumulated many positive experiences to counteract them.

Along with thinking that my dad was really smart, I didn't feel stupid about those incidents anymore. I spent the better part of a day in my room forgiving those faces I could still see in my mind. After forgiving all of them, I spent time blessing them. What my dad said gave me insight into how the experiences from my childhood could still bother or affect me now and, honestly, at times make me feel crazy.

They were lies the enemy would use often with me—"You're the only one; you're crazy; you don't fit in." The enemy often comes and reiterates all the things you already think are true. Because those self-doubts and perceptions about your faults are already within you, you give ear to that voice since there's some element of it that rings familiar. The apostle Peter warns, "Be alert and of sober mind. Your enemy the devil prowls around like a roaring lion looking for someone to devour" (1 Peter 5:8).

My relationships with the people I was encountering in my world helped to develop how I saw myself, but an even greater life-changing relationship was about to begin.

3
LEADING A CHILD

don't remember going to church when we lived in Michigan, but I remember my parents watching programs on television by ministers like Robert Schuller and Kenneth Copeland. Those programs brought about a change in my dad.

My dad believed in God, but he didn't go to church at that time. He had been let down by experiences with hypocrisy in church. Later, he received teachings and met people who seemed more real to him. About that time I began to notice a Bible around our house, a study guide, and other evidence of what was happening in his life.

Not long after we arrived in Gulf Breeze, our family joined St. Paul United Methodist Church. Dad wasn't looking for a Methodist congregation specifically, but the Lord spoke to his heart and said, "This is where your family will go to church." It was a small congregation at that time with some older ladies whose constant prayers kept the church doors open. The church eventually grew to about three hundred people. Along with home, church became the place of big encouragement for me. Over the years the people there served as heartfelt cheerleaders in my life. I felt at home being a part of church.

The children in the church kids' programs were the first kids I began to connect with when I was little. The barrier that was between me and the kids at school wasn't there with the kids at church. It was different with them for some reason. I can't say I understand that completely. It wasn't like we were sitting around having deep theological discussions. We were just interacting in an easy way, having fun together in Sunday school and on the playground.

The night I came to the Lord was during a small revival hosted by our church. The visiting revivalist doing the preaching gave an altar call. I was about nine years old and felt compelled to go forward. I walked down the aisle to the front and prayed with "Brother Doug," our young pastor, Doug Pennington. I felt his whiskers on my cheek as he leaned over the altar rail and whispered the sinner's prayer in my ear for me to say. I asked Jesus into my heart that night.

The next night at dinner I told my dad that I felt different. A big thing had happened in my life. I told Brother Doug that I wanted to be baptized right away. It was December and cold. Brother Doug tried to assure me that it would be fine to wait until the weather was warmer, but that wasn't for me. I was ready. We gathered on a boat dock at a lady's house on the Sound in the Gulf of Mexico. The weather was nasty and cold with rain and storms. Dressed in coveralls, Brother Doug lowered me into the salt water of the Sound. When I came up, it was no longer raining.

My dad became more and more involved in church and in his men's group. The men in that group met regularly, helped each other, and developed a friendship with the pastor. They knew that they needed the encouragement and support that happens in a church community. These men also knew they needed to *be* encouragement to one another and to others. It was a living example of "Let us think of ways to motivate one another to acts of love and good works. And let us not neglect our meeting together, as some people do, but encourage one another, especially now that the day of his return is drawing near" (Hebrews 10:24–25 NLT).

Dad also started listening to a minister named James Robison. He went to a few of his conferences, as well as conferences by other ministers. We began to hear about the Lord and the Bible all the time in our house. We would sit together at night after dinner while Dad read the Bible to us.

My dad's father died when my dad was three. Although my dad didn't have the example of a physical father, he embraced God as Father in such a beautiful way. He had a mom and sisters who loved him and prayed their hearts out for him. When he came into a relationship with God, it was a very real thing for him. Dad parented us from that place.

At night when we'd go to bed, Dad would play us cassette tapes in our room of teachers he had found at a James Robison conference or some other gathering. I was scared of the dark, but the voices of those teachers put me at ease. I would drift off to sleep listening to those tapes. My dad would let them continue to play even as we slept.

Dad was providing a foundation for the rest of our lives. He was putting into action "Start children off on the way they should go, and even when they are old they will not turn from it" (Proverbs 22:6).

About this same time a new program was beginning at my school. The combination of that program with the teaching about the Lord I was receiving at home would result in something I had never imagined.

4

EACH HAS HIS OWN GIFT

Many people and events speak into how we see ourselves, sometimes lifting up and sometimes pushing down the gifts in each of us.

At the beginning of sixth grade, we were given guitars in our music class at Gulf Breeze Middle School. I began learning how to play. Miss Heath, who understood about being a heavier person and was always kind to me, taught the guitar part of music class. I took to the guitar immediately, practicing and playing whenever I could. I have always enjoyed music, and I took piano lessons as a kid, but I never stuck with it. I just don't learn well that way. At the same time that I began taking an interest in playing guitar, I started making little beats on some inexpensive keyboards that I had. I also learned that I could hear music and melodies and play them on an instrument without reading printed music. My mom, of course, thought I was a genius.

When I turned twelve later that school year, my mom and dad took me to a pawn shop to buy me an electric guitar for my birthday. We found a no-name guitar for $106 and a little bitty amplifier to go with it. I had no idea that if you turn the volume control on an amp all the way up, the amp will distort and snarl at you like it does on rock records. I was just dinking around with the clean tone, playing the chords we learned in guitar class—that is, until I broke a string. The electric guitar then sat untouched for months because I didn't know where or how to get strings.

At about that same time, we visited a church called Christian International near Destin, Florida, that moved in the prophetic gifts. I'd never been around anything like that. My parents really hadn't either. That night the man preaching gave a call at the end of the service for people who would surrender to go into world missions. He said, "Anyone who feels called into the mission field, and you"— pointing directly at me—"please come down front and receive prayer." I was twelve years old and scared to death with all this talk about prophecy. I didn't know what in the world that meant or what was going to happen next. I was afraid he was going to tell my parents every bad thing I had ever done.

When I got to the front of the church, he prayed a general prayer over the group and then came and spoke directly to me. The preacher said he had seen musical notes written on my face when we were singing choruses during worship time. He said, "You are going to write songs, and one day those songs will take you far away from your home, even to a foreign land." He added that there would be people who would not like the songs but not to give them a second thought. He said I should know in my heart that I've been called by God to this.

I was so relieved he didn't tell my parents bad things I'd done that I didn't really think about the words he had just said. It was such an unexpected thing to hear, especially as I was just learning how to play music.

Not long after that, while I was still in the sixth grade, little songs started to arrive. I recorded the music part of the songs on my Casio keyboard and would sing the words accompanied by the recorded music for my friend Ben, a pastor's son. Ben still remembers the names of some of those songs to this day.

As more songs arrived, I began singing them in church—that is, except for the first time I got up to sing. I was too afraid and had to have the church pianist sing my song instead. I also came up with a few raps, which were the only songs I would perform in public at that time. Mom and Dad loved those songs because of the content. It wasn't hard-core by any means. This song was the beginning of my rapping career:

If you wanna know what's going wrong with your life
Turn to Him, He'll relieve all your strife
He's cuttin' through wrong like a two-edged knife

Repent right now, you know that the light

is gonna come back and you won't be ready

You're in sin, your faith is unsteady

Come on now, don't start to delay

Jesus is the Lord, serve Him today.

You know I'm not mean and you know I'm not lean

But I'm gonna be a fightin' machine for the King.

Super dope rhymes, huh? I was also into heavy metal. Ben and I would listen to his favorite group, Stryper, and all other kinds of Christian rock music. I'd also listen to Christian rap groups like P.I.D. (Preachers in Disguise) and the Dynamic Twins. There weren't a ton of them, but I listened to all I could get my hands on.

Along with hearing their records, I got to see Christian artists perform live. A youth pastor at our church would take us to Christian concerts all the time. The very first concert we went to see was 2nd Chapter of Acts. After that, we saw Carman. His music was different because it had a beat. What impacted me most was the message Carman delivered and the way he did it. He preached boldly. His songs were stories that he would mostly talk instead of sing. The best thing about it, though, was that he would give an altar call and people would come forward. It was great.

A long-haired dude named Mylon LeFevre and his group, Broken Heart, made an impact on me not only with their music but also with their knowledge of the Word. At the end of the concert, Mylon sat on the edge of the stage, opened the Bible, and shared the Word of God.

That resonated a lot with me. An indie band called the Newsboys had just come over from Australia and opened for them.

Besides the youth pastor who took us to concerts, others at our church encouraged music in me while ministering to our church's youth. The pianist from church and her husband were young believers who became mentors to a lot of the youth. Their house was the first place I ever saw MTV. Another youth pastor was a local beautician we called Debster. Debster was there the night the preacher gave the prophecy over me. Years later, when Big Daddy Weave played where she lives now in Anderson, South Carolina, she came to the concert and cried in the front row. These people were encouragers who made a lasting impact on me through their ministry.

All these influences had some part in shaping who I was becoming. Like a lot of people in their teenage years, I was trying to fit in and not stand out in any way. It wasn't until later in life that I learned about God's intentionality in making us all different. The apostle Paul wrote about it, saying, "Each has his own gift from God, one of one kind and one of another" (1 Corinthians 7:7 ESV) and "Having gifts that differ according to the grace given to us, let us use them" (Romans 12:6 ESV).

The enemy sometimes tries to get us to think we should hide what God made unique about us. God, however, has a plan for those qualities and abilities. Paul wrote, "For as in one body we have many members, and the members do not all have the same function, so we, though many, are one body in Christ, and individually members of one another" (Romans 12:4–5 ESV). We all have giftings that are made for the ultimate purpose of serving God and building up one another in Him.

More and more groups began performing in our area while I was in school, including the Christian metal bands I was listening to. Seeing those guys tear it up on guitar made me want to be a Christian heavy metal guitar player. My playing and songwriting abilities were growing as I absorbed what I was listening to and seeing at those concerts. The little songs that were arriving began sounding more like what I was aiming for. Music was calling on my heart stronger than ever. Now if I could only make it through high school.

5

LEARNING TO BE A FRIEND

made it through middle school and entered my freshman year at Gulf Breeze High School, where I decided to play football. Because of my size, the coaches were very interested in me coming out for the team. They said I could play on the line for the junior varsity football team. The reason I went out for football at all was because of something I saw happen with a great friend of mine who was on the team.

Players would wear their jerseys to school on game days. My friend wasn't any kind of athlete either, but I saw a cute cheerleader come up to him wearing his jersey. She and the other girls were hanging out with him. They were putting their arms around his. My friend and a lot of us were big fat boys, but that didn't seem to matter. My friend said, "Mike, you need to come do this. They love us!"

So I went out for the team, having no idea about anything to do with football. When I told my dad I was going to play football, he said, "What! Michael, you've never even watched an entire football game. Are you sure?" I told him I was absolutely sure. He said that was fine and that he and my mom would take me to practices and games. They would do whatever they needed to do to support me, but he also told me that if I joined the team, I couldn't quit. I needed to stay with it for the entire season.

Even though it was nearly time for the first game of the season, the team took me on. I had missed summer training and all the other preparations. I was terrible. The practices were so grueling that I pretended I was sick or something as often as possible.

After days of complete mystery to me, I finally got up the guts to ask another player on the team, "When the guys are out there running these plays, they're shouting numbers and colors. Then the quarterback makes this noise, and everything goes into action. How do you guys know what to do?" He said, "Weave, haven't you been getting the play sheets?"

I had absolutely no idea those pieces of paper they would hand out in the locker room were plays. I would turn them every which way, but they made no sense to me, so I just threw them away. That's how much I didn't know about football.

The football team, by the way, was where I got the name Weave. Evidently you can't have a two-syllable last name in organized sports.

I would hide during every game. I was scared to death the coach would actually put me in, but surely there was no way he'd do that. He knew I had no idea how to play football.

During the last game of the season, another guy on the team who was about my size broke his chin strap. I figured this was my chance to make it through the whole season hiding in the corner, so I threw him my helmet to use. The coach noticed and said, "Weave! That is the most selfless thing, man. I'm gonna put you in the next series."

Everything in my head went into slow motion while I screamed on the inside, "*Noooooooooooooooo!*" The coaches put me in the game. I went out there and still didn't know anything I was supposed to do. All I saw were giant dudes on the other team making grunting noises. The other team was full of guys of questionable age, like they might be college-aged guys held back to play football.

As soon as I heard all those numbers and colors yelled out, I made a beeline for the sideline. I tried to be like, "Oh man, I missed 'em!" I already had my helmet off, but the coach waved me back into the game! I did the same thing the next play. I just ran away. The coach asked me after the game if I would be coming back out the next semester. "Oh yeah!" I said.

My freshman year, however, would be my last year of public high school. I had always hated school—every moment of it. Anytime I was sick or could pretend to be sick to miss class, I would do it.

Except for the couple of classes that I had with a friend from church, I spent my time waiting for it to be the weekend.

I felt all by myself that first year of high school. I would see the people who were part of various social groups having a big time in school, and in my awkward way, I'd test the waters with them. But they would just ignore me. When one of their people came around, they would interact with them in a different way than they would with me. They dressed a certain way and liked a lot of the same things, some of which went against what I believed. My football experience was my last attempt to connect with them, but I got out there and felt more alienated than ever. No one was outright mean to me; I just couldn't connect.

I had always thought my feelings of being rejected were because of other people, but I know now they were because of me. When I felt like I wasn't connecting with someone, I would act even more awkward. I was expecting them to get past this giant hurdle I was giving them to overcome, but I was the one in the way. In this period, I began giving myself permission not to like me based on my perception of how others received me.

Part of my struggle was due to adolescence, but another part of it stemmed from the steady, long-term strategy of the enemy that began in the earliest parts of my life. His goal is our destruction, which he is happy to complete little by little over time. Jesus warns, "The thief comes only to steal and kill and destroy; I have come that they may have life, and have it to the full" (John 10:10).

I experienced a revelation when I made my first great friend that freshman year at Gulf Breeze High School. Andy Kowalchuk joined our church youth group, which made for a total of three of us. Andy was as good of a friend as a guy could have. We became great buds.

Andy's mom decided she was going to homeschool him and started a co-op. The homeschool began with Andy and a girl from our school named Kristen. Andy was in the gifted program in high school and kind of a nerd, so he didn't fit in that world either. When he graduated, he became one of the first homeschoolers to ever make it into the Air Force Academy. Andy was told he would never fly because of his eyesight, but he was not about to be stopped. He's a pilot today. I still see Andy when Big Daddy Weave plays where he lives and Andy's not flying somewhere else in the world.

With Andy, I learned that to have friends, I need to be a friend and show the sort of kindness, loyalty, and friendliness I would love to have shown to me. "Friends come and friends go, but a true friend sticks by you like family" (Proverbs 18:24 MSG).

I thought going from public school to homeschool would make my world smaller, but I never could have guessed how different the reality would be. The people I was about to meet would help open an entirely new part of my life.

6

AS ONE MAN SHARPENS ANOTHER

Around the time I started homeschooling, I began getting more and more into music. I loved it. I didn't think I was that good, but people would make a big deal whenever I sang the little songs I was writing. While that was happening, God was bringing people into my life who influenced who I was becoming as a musician. In the bigger picture, God was shaping me for how I could serve Him.

I had gotten to know a guy in our town named Perry, who was in his late twenties and had moved back home after finishing college with a master's degree in some sort of engineering. Perry played guitar and had two Ovation acoustics—an Adamas and a Balladeer twelve-string—and a Roland Jazz Chorus amp. It sounded like eight guitars at one time whenever Perry clicked on the chorus of that amp. When he played Bon Jovi's "Wanted Dead or Alive," I thought it was the greatest thing anyone had ever played in front of me on the guitar. He would sit with me and grab my finger and put it in the right place. He took time to teach me how to play.

For my fifteenth birthday, my mom, my dad, Perry, and my home-school mates Andy and Kristen threw a surprise birthday party for me. Perr, as I called him, was the shyest person in the whole world. He knew I wasn't far behind in that department, so he tipped me off right before we went inside. He said, "I would never want this to happen to me, so I'm gonna tell you, all right?" It was like I was his little brother. He said, "There's a surprise birthday party in there. Don't you dare tell anybody that you know, but I just want you to know so you're not freaked out." I kept a lid on the secret. That night I received a special gift from my mom and dad. They had bought me my first name-brand guitar, a Peavey T-60 electric.

I met a guy that night named Jody who was a little younger than Perry. He was probably about twenty years old and had recently moved to Gulf Breeze. Jody, whom we would later call Hode, was the stepbrother of a friend in our church youth group. Hode became the other big brother I never had. Since I was being homeschooled, I was available to do stuff with him. My mom was afraid he was some kind of pervert, but he was really sent by the Lord. He and I played guitar at about the same level, so we would learn together. He would take me to guitar clinics and Christian concerts.

Hode and I put together our first band with two friends from church named Trish and Kris. We called it Salvation. I played guitar and sang the lead vocal parts with the plan that I would sing until we could find a vocalist. Finding a singer never happened, which turned out to be the case for every band I have ever been a part of.

At one point, our paths crossed with a youth pastor at the local Calvary Chapel church named Roger Jahn. Roger had grown up as a guitar player, jamming with members of the Allman Brothers Band down in south Florida and playing on recording sessions in the '70s. The Lord got ahold of him and delivered him from drugs and the lifestyle that sometimes went with rock and roll. After that, he became a youth pastor. Roger told me something that stuck with me: "Man, you can play faster than I could ever hope to, but make what you're playing count. Make it sing."

Roger would sit in with us on guitar. He eventually joined our little band, playing and singing his songs, with Hode and me on guitar and Trish playing drums. Kris was on bass, but he needed to step out of the group after our first appearance when he got busier with school commitments. Since the drums were the most difficult things to move, we would all lug our stuff to Trish's house to rehearse.

A few months earlier, my brother Jay had begun learning to play bass guitar. Prior to that time he had thought playing music was kind of for sissies. He had always been the sports guy, but then music began to interest him. We went to the pawn shop and found a scaled-down bass guitar, one that's a little smaller than a normal bass. I began messing around with some slap bass ideas. Jay picked up on them and started playing bass. He was a natural. Within three months he was playing for Salvation.

Roger held an event at Calvary Chapel called Sabbath Rock. Our band Salvation became the Sabbath Rock house band. Sabbath Rock was a great outlet to try new songs and get experience playing with Roger. It was cool to have a spiritual mentor who was also a great musician. We'd also get calls to play at other places in our area, with Roger singing some of the songs and me singing others.

Even though I could sing, it stressed me out to do it. I never felt comfortable being the one out front. If only there was a way to play and hide at the same time! I had always dreamed of being the guy off to the side of the stage because I loved playing so much. Despite the stress of singing, songs would always show up that I would write and sing.

The Lord taught me a lot in that season about how we help one another grow in face-to-face personal relationships. There are ways we can grow in isolation, but there is other growth that only happens when we're in community with others. "Iron sharpens iron, and one man sharpens another" (Proverbs 27:17 ESV). It's proven to be true in my life, as the Lord used all these people to help me grow and find a voice to serve Him.

For Christmas one year I received a subscription to *CCM Magazine*. *CCM Magazine* chronicled all the happenings and artists in contemporary Christian music. Midway through the summer, after completing school and getting my GED, I opened the latest issue of CCM and saw an ad that said, "This ain't no choir tour." And brother, were they ever right.

7

SHOW ME YOUR MERCY

The ad in *CCM Magazine* was for a touring ministry group called Arc. I made a video audition to send to the founders, Chris and Marv, in Michigan. I had a friend who had an old TAC Scorpion soundboard. I sat in front of that console and played along with some popular songs while we videotaped it. One was a Rick Cua song with this ripping guitar solo on it that I played along with on the video. What I played wasn't exactly the original guitar solo, but it was close enough for the people reviewing the audition. They pumped me up, saying, "Oh man, you're great! You need to come do this."

There was one problem, however. I didn't have the look they wanted. I had grown my hair long, and that didn't fit their requirements. I was also at that awkward age, combined with my long hair and glasses, where people would sometimes have difficulty knowing how to address me. Going through the airport security line once, someone behind me began calling me, saying, "Ma'am. Ma'am." I turned around and they said, "Uh ... sir ... uh ... whatever!" My mom and my grandma thought there was no way I would be willing to cut my hair, but the hair went, and I was in.

My joining Arc broke up our band Salvation. My friend Hode, who I had learned guitar with, was a single guy who didn't have a lot of money, but he sold some things and bought me a Marshall half-stack amplifier setup to send with me. He did it just to say he believed in me and that he always had. I knew coming up with that kind of money was a huge sacrifice for him. That kind of support was a picture of real love to me.

My parents bought me a purple Ibanez RG550 electric guitar for my high school graduation present. I plugged that into a DigiTech RP-1 multi-effects unit that I ran into the Marshall half stack. Everyone made fun of me for running this dinky effects device through this amplifier with so much power, but the RP-1 had what I needed for Arc. We talked to my church and raised support, kind of missionary style, and I was ready to hit the road.

My parents and Jay drove me nearly a thousand miles in our little Ford Aerostar van from our home in Gulf Breeze, Florida, to Allegan, Michigan, where Arc was based. It was the first time I had been away from home. I stood on the doorstep crying when they left me. When I was home, I couldn't wait to leave. When I arrived, all I could think was, *What have I done?*

The first day there we put together our group. Arc 18 was our name, because ours was the eighteenth version of Arc. There was also an Arc 17 that traveled at the same time to other places. The drummer in our group was Todd Hoek from Grand Rapids, Michigan. Todd was one of the nicest guys I had ever met. He loved to play music as much as I did, and we enjoyed playing together. We became roommates. There was no bass player yet, but we jumped into learning songs like "I Swear" by All-4-One, "Livin' on the Edge" by Aerosmith, "Shine" by Collective Soul, "Why Haven't I Heard from You" by Reba McEntire, and Michael W. Smith's "Change Your World," all fun songs by popular artists at that time.

We had three separate sets of music we would play. One was a church show that included an appeal for funding and other help with Arc that was all Christian adult contemporary and inspirational songs. The second and main thing we did was a high school substance abuse awareness assembly program. It was all Top 40 songs that we felt didn't lyrically compromise our faith but that the kids would know so they could sing along. We did that set with a drama that went with it. The final thing we did was a "comeback" concert set. This concert was an evening show the kids who were at the substance abuse assembly could "come back" to. This set included songs that were mostly Christian music but would include rock and all kinds of styles. We would also preach the gospel and give an invitation.

We trained that summer and hit the road when kids were starting to go back to school. There was no false advertising to Arc's ad headline, "This ain't no choir tour." We wore the same clothes every day while we rode in a Ryder box truck and a fifteen-passenger van that was falling apart as we went down the road. We played more than three hundred fifty times in ten months, sometimes five times a day. We had to set up the gear, load it, and unload it—everything.

I met great friends in Arc, including future Big Daddy Weave production manager Matt Grunden. He was playing bass in Arc 17. Midway through touring, some of the people in our band were swapped for people in the other band. Grundy, as we call Matt, began playing with our group. Man, we had a blast.

In the middle of touring, though, Grundy injured his back and slipped a disc. The Arc organizers pulled him off the road at a time when we were close to my home. When we arrived at my house, it was the first time I had seen my parents in months.

Once again, my brother Jay was the hero. Jay learned all of Grundy's parts in one night during a ride in the van to the next event. Jay was a hyperactive guy and was active on stage like no one else had been. He would jump and spin one place, then run to another spot and jump off something. One time while playing "Livin' on the Edge," Jay jumped in the air, and in mid-spin, the wireless instrument pack connected to his bass flew off his guitar and smacked a kid in the front row right in the face. Jay has remained primarily stationary on stage ever since.

The first girl I ever fell for was in our group. I thought she was beautiful. As we were getting to know each other on the road, something started between us. I told her how I felt about her, and we got close. We had so many things in common. After we had been technically dating for about three months, we played in her town. I liked her so much that I got up the gumption to talk to her dad about how serious I was about this relationship. To my surprise, it was the first time he had heard anything about us!

After Arc ended, I was still crazy about this girl. I went to see her at her home in South Carolina. One night not long after I arrived, her parents sent her to break up with me. They had highlighted sections in a book they were reading that talked about why their daughter could never marry a guy who was overweight.

That destroyed me. It was late at night when this happened. I decided to drive home to Florida from South Carolina right then and there. I called Jay, who said, "Don't do it. Don't go. Hang out until the morning, get straight, and then come back." I came home so defeated.

I know God is good and that He is present, but it was still so hard not to feel utterly alone. Even David, someone who knew the Lord so closely, felt this: "Come, Lord, and show me your mercy, for I am helpless, overwhelmed, in deep distress" (Psalm 25:16 TLB). I was hurting so bad.

Toward the end of that summer, Chris and the guys at Arc had me back up to Michigan to help get the next year's groups ready. Even though that girl wasn't in Arc anymore, I saw her in my mind everywhere I looked. I was completely devastated.

8

IN THE POWER OF SIGNS AND WONDERS

People back home were praying that God would direct me. They didn't think I was supposed to go on tour for another year with Arc, and I didn't either. It just wasn't the same. I helped the Arc team in Michigan get ready for the next tour and then returned to Florida.

I was still dealing with the pain and hurt. At least at home in Gulf Breeze I was surrounded by support. My pastor even created an opportunity for me to lead worship at church. There was one big catch: He made it a requirement of the job that I had to be at least a part-time college student. That was a tough one. I never had plans to go to college. Playing music for a living was all I ever wanted to do for as long as I could remember. I just didn't know how to make a career out of it.

Since it was a job requirement, I applied for school at Pensacola Junior College. I was afraid I might not get in because I didn't have a traditional knowledge of performing or reading music. Everything I did was all by ear. When I visited the school to apply for a music scholarship, they asked me what I wanted to pursue. I didn't say guitar, because I loved playing guitar. I never wanted the guitar to become work. I wanted to keep the guitar fun. I tried out for voice instead, thinking my ear could carry me. It also seemed like it would be easier to memorize a single line of music as opposed to six strings. After my tryout, Pensacola Junior College offered me a partial scholarship. My college career was on its way.

Even as a young man in junior college, I was still afraid every day. I also didn't really want to be there. I would skip most classes due to my anxiety. I would sing and do what I had to do, but most of the teachers didn't really care if I was there or not. I wouldn't do most of the homework, but I did well enough on the tests to get a grade that would be passing.

Along with classes, I was leading worship at church. I was now singing as well as playing. I wasn't as afraid to sing when we led worship. I could close my eyes and sing to God while at the same time encouraging other people to worship.

A significant career event happened for me one Sunday when

I led worship while playing electric guitar. One day of that was enough for my pastor. The clean electric guitar sound was too twangy for him, so he gave me some money and sent me to buy an acoustic guitar. I found a Takamine acoustic and have been playing acoustic guitar ever since.

My playing outside of church also took a turn. When I was in Arc, we played in so many cities where we had to unload and load in snow, which made those days much tougher. I told our Arc drummer, Todd, that if we ever got out of Arc alive, we'd go to snowless Florida, start a band called Down South, and stay there. Eventually Todd came to Florida, moved in with us, and that's what we did. We had a three-piece group and were writing primarily hard rock songs. I was leading worship, Todd was working construction, and the rest of the time we put our creative energies into Down South with my brother Jay on bass.

The most significant turn in my life at that time, however, went beyond playing music. In nearby Pensacola, the Brownsville Revival was drawing millions of people from all over the world. Lindell Cooley was leading worship there using songs from a Vineyard Music series called Touching the Father's Heart. The series featured songs from various worship leaders who were writing about knowing God and being in an intimate relationship with Him.

There were so many things about the revival and that setting I didn't understand, but I did see people who had been touched by God and were now walking in intimacy with Him. Todd was one of them. He went over to the Brownsville Revival and had a significant encounter with the Lord that got me going back there just about every night for weeks. Todd had gotten smacked to the floor in some kind of spiritual way and lay there for hours. He had never even heard of that kind of thing happening, so I knew he wasn't putting on an act.

Steve Hill had just given an altar call. Todd ran down the aisle but never made it to the front. He fell to the floor and remained there for over two and a half hours. He was laughing and crying, but he couldn't get up. At about 1:00 a.m., long after the preaching had finished, people were still there worshipping. I had to get someone to help me put Todd in a wheelchair. We got him out into the parking lot and put him in my Honda Prelude. Todd was still out of it.

When we got home, I needed my dad's help to get Todd out of the car. We got him inside as best we could and laid him facedown on the bed. About fifteen minutes later, Todd came out to use the restroom. After that day, he was never the same. There was a fire in him for God that would express itself in the craziest ways. It would just show up in a room, like Paul wrote about coming "in the power of signs and wonders, in the power of the Spirit" (Romans 15:19 NASB). There was an authority on it that filled whatever space in which it appeared. "For our gospel did not come to you in word only, but also in power and in the Holy Spirit and with full conviction" (1 Thessalonians 1:5 NASB).

Not long after that night, our church youth group came back from a weekend retreat. These were usually pretty emotional events. This group of kids, however, were so hard that they were unmoved by any of it. Todd came with us to meet with the kids the night they returned. After the youth pastor finished talking with the kids and was about to dismiss them, Todd asked if he could say something. The pastor said sure, go ahead. All Todd said was, "I just want you to know that Jesus Christ died for your sins, and He's the only way to get to heaven after this life is over. In case something happens to you or whatever, I just wanted you to know that. That's all." He said it just like that and sat down.

Kids began weeping. They hugged one another, just holding on to each other. They went home, woke up their parents, and told them about bad things they'd been into and repented. I thought to myself, *What in the world has happened? Whatever happened to Todd, I gotta get that.*

9

THE PLANS
I HAVE FOR YOU

I went back to Brownsville night after night. Dudes were shouting as they prayed for me while I heard people nearby making noises that sounded like barking. It was unlike any kind of church experience I'd had before, but nothing ever happened to me like it did to Todd. Something dawned on me, though. In continually going back each night, seeking that thing that Todd experienced and being in that environment, I was starting to think differently. My mind was being transformed. It was God's presence that was doing that.

The worship happening at Brownsville was from a place of intimacy with God. That introduced me to something I had never experienced—an intimacy with God *through* music. Prior to that, I had been playing to impress somebody and then give God glory, or to impress someone long enough so they would listen to me share a message with them. The people at Brownsville were literally singing to God. That idea shaped what would become Big Daddy Weave.

With all that was going on, I became distracted. I wasn't keeping up with my studies like my pastor thought I should be. He told me about a four-year college close by called the University of Mobile. It was far enough away that I couldn't be at church every day, but close enough for me to be able to come home on the weekends.

My first week at the University of Mobile came with a huge amount of anxiety. I was so nervous about being around that many peers that I might as well have been back in elementary school. I was feeling the exact same things I'd felt back then. Even after playing all those shows with Arc, the issues in my life that had never been dealt with were still as powerful as ever.

The students at the University of Mobile weren't even real-world cool kids. They were just your average Baptist kids. My perception of them, though, still made me turn on my weird and alienate myself from them. I thought for years that it was their doing, but I know now it was all me.

One of the first classes I had on campus was Music Theory. It was second-year Music Theory because I had already finished up a couple of semesters in community college. Joseph Shirk was one of the first guys I met in that class. His reputation as a singer and saxophone player preceded him. From my perspective, he was one of the cool kids. Everyone talked about him—"Oh, that's Joe. He plays the sax. Have you heard him play? He's great."

Dave Matthews' music was all over the radio at that time. A lot of their songs featured saxophone parts that helped make those records special. I thought sounds like that could work well with what I was writing. I got up the nerve to approach Joe in class about it. I told him I thought sax would sound great on a couple of songs I'd written and mentioned a few of the current influences on my music. It turned out he was listening to some of those same records. That got his attention. Joe said, "I'd like to hear those sometime," to which I replied, "I have my guitar in the hallway. How about now?"

We went into the hall, I grabbed my case, and we stepped into an open practice room. I got out my acoustic guitar and began playing song ideas for him. Joe's roommate, Ben George, was a drummer and was walking down the hall at the time with another drummer. When Ben overheard me playing a song I'd written called "Pharisee," his ears perked up. Ben hustled the other drummer into an elevator to eliminate any competition and stepped into the practice room to see what this was about. Joe was surprised. He hadn't expected to hear music like that from someone at our school.

Joe heard enough of something in those first songs to interest him. Jay and I had been recording demos of songs I had written at our church in Gulf Breeze. The two of us were now leading worship there together. I invited Joe over to the church to record. Just like I thought he would, Joe played great and added something unique to those recordings.

That went well enough that we arranged a time to have our first jam session together. We made a plan for Joe to invite Ben George to play drums and for me to invite Jay to play bass. We scheduled a time to meet one afternoon at Martin Hall in the music building on the University of Mobile campus. It was our first time to jam and play together, and, man, was it fun! Those guys liked the same kind of stuff that I did. We were all listening to artists like Sting, Bruce Hornsby, and Béla Fleck.

After no more than fifteen minutes of playing, two students involved with the student council event planning committee came into the room. Their committee had been meeting in the same building and had heard the noise we were making downstairs. They told us they were planning Ramfest, the school homecoming event. "We have a band booked to play it," they said, "but you guys need to come open for them." We said okay. We had only been together fifteen minutes and we had our first gig!

We were asked what our band name was so they could put it on the flyer for the show. Jay and I had been messing around with a name as a joke, and as a laugh, I told them to call us Big Daddy Weave and the Institution. Joe and Ben looked at me like, "What is *that*?" We all had a big laugh. Before we knew it, though, that name was on all kinds of things, and that was that. For better or for worse, we were branded.

The day for our first performance arrived, our debut at the University of Mobile's Ramfest. We performed three original songs called "In Christ," "Pharisee," and an instrumental we called "The Funk." We also played "Hold Me Jesus" by Rich Mullins. We opened for a group that day with an equally weird name. It was a band known as Dog Named David. We had no way to know at the time that two of the players in that group would become a significant part of our lives.

I love how the Lord uses anything and everything for His kingdom. Despite all our efforts and floundering around sometimes, God says, "For I know the plans I have for you . . . plans to prosper you and not to harm you, plans to give you hope and a future" (Jeremiah 29:11).

10

THOSE WHO KNOW YOU TRUST IN YOU

I was hearing other students at the University of Mobile talk about a music performance major studying classical guitar named Jeremy Redmon. They said he was this great musician who could play in all kinds of alternate tunings. At the time Jeremy was playing bass in Dog Named David, which was gaining in popularity in our area. They had reached a place where our band felt privileged to open for them. The two main members of that group, however, were asked to perform as an acoustic duo opening for an even bigger band at the time, Caedmon's Call. That left Jeremy and Dog Named David's drummer, Jeff Jones, without a band.

Jeff had already graduated from the University of Mobile with a major in psychology. He was going to be the next Dr. Dobson. Jeff also had ambitions of becoming a country music songwriter. He would come over to our apartment and play us songs he'd written with titles like "Stop, Drop, and Roll into Your Lovin' Arms Tonight." As much as he liked psychology and songwriting, Jeff loved playing the drums even more. He could re-create ridiculously difficult drum fills played by accomplished players like Carter Beauford of the Dave Matthews Band.

Not long after the breakup of Dog Named David, Jeff Jones hired us to play with him at an event for his brother. He also separately hired Jeremy Redmon to run sound using the PA gear Jeremy owned. It was at the event for Jeff's brother that Jeremy and I really got to know each other.

The University of Mobile was different from junior college. This school was more serious about the students being present in the classroom. That only aggravated my uneasiness around other people. The boldness to take out my acoustic guitar in the music building in front of God and everybody and show Joe Shirk those first songs was a highly unusual event.

My anxiety was so bad that if I thought a teacher was going to call on me to talk in front of people, I would leave the classroom. Just the thought of it would make me feel short of breath, like the room was closing in on me. I would sweat and urgently feel like I had to leave.

One of my standard exit strategies was to act like I needed to sharpen my pencil. I would only take my pencil with me, leaving my books and everything else behind. I would just walk out and not come back until class was over.

Sometimes I would wander down the hallway to where Jeremy Redmon was hanging out in an oversized wicker chair during his free period. I'd say, "Hey, dude, what are you doing?" He would respond, "Nothing, man. I've got a free period." And I'd say, "Let's turn your free period into a lunch period!" Then we would get into his navy blue Ford Explorer and go to lunch. I would do that anytime I would see him out there and he was willing to go. We got to know each other well during those free/lunch periods.

Jay, who around this time I began calling Jay Dawg, wasn't enrolled at the University of Mobile, but he was always there. I was even told by the school, "You know, Mike, he can't live with you in campus housing." That inspired us to get our own place.

Jay, our friend Ben George, and I moved into a small duplex apartment in Mobile. When nobody was home in the adjoining unit, we would set up Ben's drums and jam. We enjoyed playing together so much that we could jam over the same song for hours on end. Joe was busy with school but would find time to get away and join us when he could.

Jeremy Redmon came by one day, sat down at a keyboard, and began playing a funky riff he'd come up with. I immediately told Joe to get on it and double what Jeremy was playing. It was so much fun. We played that thing for hours. That riff eventually became the beginning of our song "Never Goin' Back." We probably sounded terrible, but we loved it. That was the day Jeremy Redmon joined Big Daddy Weave.

Over the next few months, with Jeremy and me on acoustic guitar, Joe on saxophone, Jay on bass, and Ben on drums, our band started playing a few events. During that time, even though we were and are all still buddies, Jay, Joe, Jeremy, and I were seeing some things differently than Ben. When Ben eventually moved back to Illinois, we invited Jeff Jones to be our drummer.

That group of guys became Big Daddy Weave for many years to come. There was a similarity to each of our backgrounds. We all grew up in church. We had never tried to pursue music outside of church. We all had hearts for the Lord. We all just wanted to be involved in music that genuinely honored God. Our relationships with one another were coming from that common ground.

My experiences leading worship, the realization at Brownsville of the intimacy with the Lord that could be experienced in a music setting, and the five of our lives being joined were all coming together in this thing called Big Daddy Weave. I knew music could set the stage for intimacy with God, but I was learning that intimacy with God can take place *through* the music itself. Our desire was to "be filled with the Holy Spirit, singing psalms and hymns and spiritual songs among yourselves, and making music to the Lord in your hearts" (Ephesians 5:18–19 NLT).

As Big Daddy Weave, we became involved in leading worship for our school's chapel—in, ironically, Weaver Hall. We would also play other events and concerts on campus. Because of the University of

Mobile's affiliation with Southern Baptist churches, lots of our fellow students were either going into internships at churches or were graduating and being hired into ministry programs of all types. We would then get calls from those people who were now in local churches and knew us from school to come and play their youth group gatherings and other events.

We'd go anywhere people would call us to play, even if it was extremely awkward. We played at a used car lot. We played a wedding reception at a Chinese buffet. People had a few drinks at that one and were dancing a little too wildly. Jeff Jones was laughing out loud because he'd never seen anyone booty dance before to the song "Trading My Sorrows." More often than not, we'd play at youth weekends or retreats. During the summer we would be busy with week-long camps.

We made an agreement not to call anyone to find a place to play. We all had seen enough people go absolutely broke chasing the dream. We said, "Lord, if this is what You want us to do, You bring the shows and we'll play them."

"Those who know your name trust in you, for you, LORD, have never forsaken those who seek you" (Psalm 9:10).

11

DIRECTING OUR PATHS

Big Daddy Weave was being asked to play so often that my mom had to start taking the phone calls from people wanting to book us. Anyone in the band who didn't have a class would play the Saraland First Assembly on Wednesday nights for their youth group. We would get $25 each for that. As a college student I thought that was great! We got about the same for playing Sunday night worship at Dauphin Way Baptist Church. Then we'd play a college and career night at Olive Baptist Church in Pensacola on Tuesdays. Those little weekly gigs in addition to the camps and other events filled our weeks. By the end of our third year together, we were playing 180 dates per year and hadn't called a single person to book us.

Another campus event we did was lead worship for a speaker named Dwight Singleton during Spiritual Emphasis week. We would lead worship, Dwight would give an altar call, and people would respond to it. I thought in my heart, *This is exactly what I was made for.* With that conviction growing in me and seeing what was happening at our shows, I began to wonder why I was going to college. I was spending all this money and not learning anything that was helping me do what was in my heart to do. Jeff had already finished college, Jeremy graduated next, but I knew my time in college was coming to a close.

When we weren't playing, we were recording. Our friend Dave Gillette opened his multimillion-dollar recording studio to us to use for free. We spent about a year hanging out there and recording between gigs. We learned so much during that time. It was an incredible opportunity for guys like us who didn't know anything to have the access and time to learn how to record on Dave's top-of-the-line equipment. At the end of that year we had completed an independent album produced by our own Jeremy Redmon we called *Neighborhoods.* Jeremy had produced some other little projects, but I had never seen him work so hard on anything before. He would stay in the studio for days, sometimes working so hard that it just about made him sick.

Just as recording a record was becoming possible for people to do on their own, the way CDs could be distributed was starting to change as well. Our independent album was finished at about the same time a new website called Grassroots Music began to distribute music online. This was a very new thing. Now something you created could be released for sale on the internet. Kent Vancil, a friend of ours, worked at a Family Christian bookstore. He had kept me up-to-date on the latest Christian heavy metal bands when I was a teenager and was a big encourager of Big Daddy Weave. Kent sent our CD to the Grassroots Music folks, who began to carry a few copies of our album.

I didn't know this at the time, but some of the record companies were starting to find out about emerging artists on the Grassroots Music site. It wasn't long before we began getting calls from record labels. When we'd make a stop in Nashville, we would talk with some of the labels who called us, like Reunion Records and Squint Records. When we went to Mobile, we had lunch with Integrity Records.

Not long after those meetings, I got a call from a woman named Susan Riley at Fervent Records. It sounded like the business was in someone's basement. It seemed so much like it wasn't a real thing that I didn't even call her back the first three times she called. She tried a couple more times until we finally connected.

Susan was so sweet and said how much she liked us. It wasn't at all what you'd expect from the president of a record company. She shared that she and her husband, Rod, had started a label and wanted to fly out to see us play. Right after that, they came and saw us perform at the Heights Baptist Church in Dallas, Texas. We instantly loved them. They're the sweetest and kindest people, the most real, everyday folks. As a result of meeting with them, we entertained the thought for the first time of signing with a record label.

Previously we didn't want to sign because the business side of music terrified us. We were sure it would mean making compromises to what God wanted to do with the music. Big Daddy Weave was already performing more than a lot of other people, including artists who were on record labels, and our audience was growing. We felt like we owed all the control to the Lord. We didn't want to give any of that control to a record label.

We started talking about contracts with Rod and Susan. It immediately scared all of us to death. The deal they were describing sounded terrible. "We've got to recoup a recording budget from 12 percent? Twelve percent of what? How does that sound like a good deal?" At one point, we called everyone and told them no thanks. We didn't want to string anyone along. We just wanted to do the right thing in front of God.

The last call I made was to Rod Riley at Fervent. He just thanked us for talking to them. When I hung up the phone with Rod, I felt sick. With everyone else I felt relief, but I felt terrible after telling Rod and Susan we didn't want to sign with them.

During this time we opened for one of the greatest indie bands there was at the time, MercyMe. They had a bus, they had insurance, and they had salaries. Everything was legit. We thought they had reached the top of the mountain compared to all the junk we were enduring. After hearing how they did it without a record company, we decided we could get away with never having to sign a contract with a record label.

Then we found out that MercyMe was signing a record deal after all. We were sure they were throwing everything away. I called Bart Millard and asked why they'd do that. He shared with me for an hour all the reasons they had made that decision. He also said that if MercyMe hadn't already been in negotiations with the people they were signing with, they would have gone with Rod and Susan.

Right about that same time, a speaker we had worked with gave our CD to Jeromy Deibler from the group FFH. We were hearing FFH songs on the radio about every fifteen minutes. Jeromy found our number and called us. He'd been running to our music in the mornings. He said he loved our indie record and offered his help.

Even though I felt so flaky after having told everybody no, I went to the other Big Daddy Weave guys, told them about my conversation with Bart, and shared what he said. I let them know I thought we had missed what we were supposed to do. I called Rod and Susan back and told them I was wrong.

Something was happening, and I didn't want to miss the Lord. These words were especially meaningful for us at that time in our lives: "Trust in the LORD with all your heart; do not depend on your own understanding. Seek his will in all you do, and he will show you which path to take" (Proverbs 3:5–6 NLT).

12

THOSE WHO WAIT WILL RENEW THEIR STRENGTH

My brother, Jay, and I were both single and back living at home with our parents, who by this time were helping run the Big Daddy Weave office. We had become traveling bros from all of the Big Daddy Weave shows we were playing who were excited for our next big journey, driving to Nashville to meet with Rod and Susan Riley at Fervent Records.

We woke up that morning and got ready to hit the road. The date was September 11, 2001. Just as we were finishing breakfast, we saw the tragedy at the Twin Towers. At first we didn't comprehend the significance of what had happened, but the implications of it slowly set in. We went ahead and left while still absorbing this weight that had fallen over the entire country.

At the end of this heavy day, we showed up for our dinner at the Green Hills Grille in Nashville. Randomly, Michael W. Smith walked into the restaurant. I freaked out. We didn't see artists like Michael W. Smith come into restaurants in Gulf Breeze.

We sat down with the people from Fervent Records and shared what God was doing. Rod and Susan introduced us to everyone on the Fervent staff that night, including one of their interns, Kandice Kirkham. I thought she was the prettiest girl I'd ever seen. Little did I know that on the day the rest of the world was falling apart, God was ordering my steps. He was on the way to blessing me more than I could ever deserve, and that doesn't even begin to cover it. I love that the Lord brings life in the midst of destruction. In the middle of the deep darkness of that day, Kandice Kirkham was sitting in front of me.

The greatest thing about that night and the only part of the talk I remember is that somebody said something about peeing in the shower. At a table full of people, Kandice owned up to doing it. I literally didn't think you could be that pretty and pee in the shower. That was the beginning of knowing I loved her, since that's just the kind of thing I would say.

Kandice was hired as the marketing director for Fervent. Fervent Records was incredible, due in part to its day-to-day operations being run by three girls in their twenties. I'd never seen anyone work so hard. Kandice and I would get to know each other well because we would have to do all kinds of promotional things together.

I really liked Kandice, but I always felt so awkward around girls. I took a bold step and summoned the courage to ask her, just hypothetically, if she would ever consider dating an artist. I didn't know it at the time, but the girls in the Fervent office had been prodding Kandice to date a guy in one of the other groups signed to the label. When I asked her if she would ever date an artist, she thought I was talking about that guy. Based on that, she gave an emphatic no. I took it as her saying I didn't have a shot. I had already been crushed by my experience with the girl I cared for back in the Arc days, so I wasn't going to go there again.

After that, it was great. All the weirdness went away. She was just this girl I really appreciated. We became friends who would talk about real life. There were hardly any other girls I was that comfortable with. We just had a good time talking. My mom got to know Kandice through their business conversations. She told my dad that she wished I would find a sweet young lady like Kandice. The Lord is so neat like that.

Jay and I were sent on radio promotion tours with Kandice. Those were great times spent with her, this sweet young lady taking these two gnarly guys around. We went all over the US on that promo tour for the first record, shaking hands, kissing babies, pouring coffee, the works. We made so many friends in Christian radio that way.

Jay had been seeing his girlfriend Emily during this time. While Kandice, Jay, and I were riding in the car together on that initial promo tour, Emily called Jay and broke it off with him. His deep chest sobs, the kind you can't hide, were so hard to hear. Kandice and

I were in the front seat of the car. It was very awkward, but we were hurting for him.

Soon after that, the song "In Christ," our first single released to radio, became a hit. About that same time, Emily started coming back around. I got super defensive about that, but then she went to my mom and apologized. I thought that was a big move on her part because Emily is quiet and private. My mom laid it out for her. She told Emily that if she was thinking about coming back into Jay's life, she needed to be ready to make a commitment to him, because that's how he felt about her. She said she loved him totally.

When Jay married Emily, it was a lonely day for me. I felt like my best friend in the world was gone. But I only felt that way for a little while. One of the great joys of my life is still getting to be with Jay in Big Daddy Weave.

That next season of life was weird and lonely. There is a cool thing about weird and lonely seasons, though. You find the Lord in those places. I love that. It sounds crazy, but my weird and lonely seasons have turned out to be the greatest blessings of my life because that's when I turned to Him.

I wish my normal days would be filled with turning to Him. He's always available to us, but we don't always see Him until we're desperate. I wish I could hold on to Him all the time. The Lord offers so much more than we even think to ask. Isaiah wrote:

Have you not known? Have you not heard? The LORD is the everlasting God, the Creator of the ends of the earth. He does not faint or grow weary; his understanding is unsearchable. He gives power to the faint, and to him who has no might he increases strength. Even youths shall faint and be weary, and young men shall fall exhausted; but they who wait for the Lord shall renew their strength; they shall mount up with wings like eagles; they shall run and not be weary; they shall walk and not faint. (Isaiah 40:28–31 ESV)

It doesn't get any more powerful than that. Who wouldn't want access to that every day? I started walking that track, talking to Jesus about being lonely and wanting something more. The Lord began to meet me there.

13
ESTABLISHING OUR STEPS

I liked a girl around that time who worked at our church, but it wasn't working out at all. The Lord began to show me that I wasn't supposed to seek her in that way. I was to pursue Him instead. The Lord showed me a date on the calendar six months away and told me that on that date I was supposed to ask her something. The only part I didn't know was *what* I was supposed to ask her. I thought I might be led to propose, but I didn't know.

I began writing on my arm with a permanent marker how many days it was until that day. I was pursuing the Lord each day, looking toward that date, walking through this time with my pastor and telling him all about it. In the meantime I was spending all my money and time trying to be good to this girl and be her friend.

Throughout this period, I was going after the Lord in a big way. I was also dropping a bunch of weight and getting into a healthy place. In the fall of 2004, it was time to go on another run of radio promo visits to support the release of our new record. This time it was just me and Kandice. There wasn't anything weird about that for me. I had tried approaching her before and had been shut down. I didn't think I had a shot in the world. However, whenever she dropped me off at the end of a run of radio visits to fly home or to a show, I missed her immediately. I didn't know it at the time, but Kandice was feeling the same way.

Meanwhile, Big Daddy Weave was traveling all over the country on tour with the group FFH. Jeromy Deibler from FFH had produced our first record for Fervent, and radio had embraced it. Our first single, "In Christ," went to number two on the Christian Adult Contemporary chart, the main radio chart for Christian music.

As great as that was, we thought the ride was over when our second single, "Audience of One," didn't perform well at AC radio. But then, while on our first big tour opening for Rebecca St. James, people began cheering loudly whenever we played it. We wondered what in the world was going on. "Audience of One" was making a slow climb up the Contemporary Hit Radio chart, another Christian radio format. A year after it was released, it became the number one song on the CHR chart. It ultimately became the second most played song at CHR that year. That's so awesome to me because that song was written while we were cleaning toilets at our church.

Months passed. It was now September. The day I was supposed to ask the girl from our church the unknown question was quickly approaching. Our tour bus was parked in a Kroger parking lot in Nashville. We were hanging out watching the Weather Channel because Hurricane Ivan was building and approaching where we lived. There was some question about whether the roads leading to our home would even be passable.

We were about ready to head for home when I got a call from Kandice. Kandice brought up our talks about the girl in Florida. It hadn't been going well, so I had been getting advice from Kandice about how to position myself to ask this girl this mystery question. Kandice had been hearing my heart and had been thinking about my situation with the other girl. She told me she was glad it wasn't working out since that would ruin her shot with me.

I was frozen in shock. I was unable to answer, unable to even respond to her. As I was outside standing behind the bus listening to her tell me this, my thoughts were a blur. One thought was that this was happening the wrong way. The dude should be saying this to the girl. The more shocking thought was that this was Kandice, who is so wonderful, saying these words to me. I was flabbergasted that a relationship with her was even a possibility.

My silence made Kandice think she had crossed a line and ruined our friendship. All I could finally get out was that I needed to call her back. I got back on the bus, walked past everyone in a zombie-like state, climbed into my bunk, and stared at the ceiling trying to process what had just happened. Within two weeks of the date the Lord had told me to wait for, He put Kandice's revelation in my way.

I called my pastor, Pastor Jay, and told him what had happened. He told me right away that he thought there was something to this. I just lay there feeling that if there was, I was the last one to know it. Our keyboard player, Joe Shirk, had once said something about noticing something between Kandice and me. I had told him I had no shot, but he was skeptical.

Pastor Jay said I should get off the bus, call her back, and find out what was going on. Hurricane Ivan was now making landfall. Our town of Gulf Breeze and the roads leading to it were closed. I decided I should stay in Nashville. I didn't tell the guys what was going on, which is very uncharacteristic of me. I just said that I needed to get off the bus to do something in Nashville. Everyone went with it.

I got a hotel room and called Kandice back. I apologized for not being able to respond to her appropriately. I told her I thought it was an awesome idea and asked her out to a movie. Of course, it was all backward again, because I was in Nashville, her town, without a car so she had to pick me up. All I had was dirty underwear from the road. I was spraying everything with cologne. I was so nervous, but I was ecstatic. It was awesome and terrible.

Kandice came and picked me up to go to the movie. We sat across from each other outside before it was time to go in the theater. I just looked at her and couldn't talk. After the movie, we went to dinner and met a couple of her friends who were dating to play mini golf.

Every bit of it was so awkward. When Kandice got in the car and left that night, she didn't think it was going to work out. She felt like bringing it out in the open had changed everything. We weren't at ease with each other like we used to be.

Later that night my parents called and told me shocking news. Hurricane Ivan brought a storm surge caused by fifty-two-foot waves that hit our little community in Gulf Breeze, bringing horrifying destruction to many parts of the town. Our family lost everything.

I rented a car and immediately made the trip back home to Florida. When I arrived, I saw that everything at our house had been damaged. My parents had moved my car, so that was saved, but that was it. We couldn't even get into our house at first. The house was filled with so much water that even the furniture had moved. Jay was finally able to pry open the sliding glass door. When he did, a snake came slithering out of our house.

Our neighborhood looked like a war zone. It was so odd. So many random items were in our front yard that we couldn't even see the ground—pieces of boat docks, appliances, toilets. It was hard to think of how to even start to clean it up.

This was all right around the date the Lord told me I was supposed to call the girl at my church and ask her something. To be faithful to that word, I called and talked with her. I asked her what she thought about me. Her response was lukewarm, so I was like, okay! I had asked her, and that was that. I was thrilled, because now I could explore what this new turn of events with Kandice might mean.

After losing their house, my parents moved in with Jay and

his wife, Emily. Jay and Emily had just found out that they were expecting their first child. Their house was full. I had this new thing happening with Kandice in Nashville, so I packed up my 2002 Ford Expedition with my laundry from the road and my guitars that had been with me on tour. I got behind the wheel with everything I had left in the world and headed to Nashville.

I lost everything in Florida but found everything at the same time. For years I had sworn I would never move to Nashville because I hated the business part of the music business, but God had different plans for me. My life was the classic example of "The heart of man plans his way, but the Lord establishes his steps" (Proverbs 16:9 ESV). Thank You, Lord, for that!

14

WORKING IN EVERY CIRCUMSTANCE

I was instantly and unexpectedly transplanted from my comfort zone of the small town of Gulf Breeze, Florida—with the people I had known nearly all my life and my local church culture—to the big city of Nashville, Tennessee. In Florida, our circle of friends thought what we did was special. In Nashville, lots of people did what we were doing. In my mind, it was a place full of people who, if they didn't do what you did better, there was a good chance they thought they did. Emotionally, this move put me in high school all over again.

Just four months after that day in September when Kandice shocked my world in such a wonderful way, we became engaged. It was December of 2004. I tell people there was a two-week window of opportunity when balding, overweight worship leaders were "in" in Nashville. We closed the deal quick, fast, and in a hurry. We married in May of 2005.

The first year of marriage is such a shock in many ways. My being on the road all the time added an additional challenge to our first year of married life. Trying to merge two lives is a stressful thing, especially when one person (in our case, Kandice) is very secure in who she is, and the other person (me) is not. If Kandice feels threatened, she'll say so. She's very vocal about it. I'm so insecure, I don't even know how to express myself much of the time. It was frustrating not knowing what was driving that insecurity in me.

One thing I didn't want to do was hang out with people. Kandice, who was very plugged in to her world in Nashville, had great and deep friendships. Some of her friends I knew and would talk to on a regular basis, but I had never hung out with them. I put stress on Kandice and me by not wanting to spend time with anyone but her.

The awkwardness that had followed me since grade school was ever present and preventing me from connecting with anyone. Being with Kandice alone, though, was another story. I had always felt like it was such a treat to be with her from the very beginning. Because I thought there was no chance for us as a couple in our earliest days of knowing each other, there was always an ease between us that continues through this day.

As strong and confident as Kandice is, her life story also contains tragedy that is still painful. Sometime before we were married,

Kandice and I were enjoying lunch together at one of our favorite Mexican restaurants. During our conversation, she told me about losing her mom when she was a child. Even though she was completely composed and smiling while pouring her heart out to me, I could see how much this tragic loss was still haunting her. I was hurting deeply for Kandice as she told me what happened.

Kandice and I had opportunities to learn more about each other at a deeper emotional level during premarital counseling with our amazing friend Al Andrews. One of the wonderful qualities about Al is his honesty. He told us there's no perfect way to prepare for marriage, and that premarital counseling would just be a gradual unveiling of who we really are. For me, Al's words led to some introspection I had never opened myself to before. In my church experience, you didn't do that. You just needed to do what the Bible said. But what if you didn't?

We met together weekly with Kandice and I taking turns talking, she sharing things on her heart one week, and I doing the same the following week. She would cry one session, and I'd cry the next. When Al asked Kandice about her childhood, she shared about losing her mom to leukemia. She recalled months at a time when she could only see her mom through a glass window but couldn't touch her. There was so much hoping and praying for her mother and their family.

I once had the occasion to meet speaker and author Beth Moore. Beth and Kandice's mom, Sandra, were childhood friends. She said she remembered the Kirkham girls, Kandice and her sisters, and she remembered praying for Kandice's mom. When healing never came this side of heaven, Beth remembered praying for the Kirkham children.

Kandice shared with Al and me about the morning after the funeral. Her only understanding of how a family worked was based on the show *Little House on the Prairie*. When a mom on that show died, the next morning it was the oldest daughter's job to take over. Kandice's grandmother came into the kitchen the morning after Kandice's mom died and saw Kandice cleaning and making breakfast for the family. Her grandmother asked what she was doing. Kandice said this was her job now. She was in the fifth grade.

While telling this story, Kandice had that same smile on her face that she had the first time she told it to me. When she finished, Al asked her if she had ever told that story without smiling. She broke down weeping.

While Kandice's mother was undergoing treatment, and in the days after her mom passed, Kandice and her sisters would stay with other families. Christian singer Wayne Watson and his wife were one of those families that opened their home to the girls. Kandice's mom had fought a long battle. Everyone had been praying and fighting for her for so long. Wayne wrote a song from the experience that became one of his biggest records, "Home Free." That song is about Kandice's mom. It's dedicated to the Kirkham family in the album liner notes. Kandice would often help out at Wayne's shows, where people would approach her and tell her how much that song meant to them. It made a little bit of sense out of something that had threatened to destroy them.

God is working in every circumstance, in every single aspect of the universe. I've seen in my life with Kandice that an area of strength in the natural world is sometimes pointing to a weakness or brokenness. The fact that I'm happy-go-lucky sometimes destroys us, and at other times it makes me Superman. The idea that she's so structured holds my flightiness together, but that same thing can sometimes drive her into the ground.

Learning to unveil who we really are is a giant step toward becoming who God designed us to be. When we're honest with both ourselves and God and pull back the layers, we can die to self. If Paul were speaking about me specifically, he might say, "Mike has been crucified with Christ. It's no longer Mike who lives, but Christ who lives in Mike" (Galatians 2:20, my paraphrase). I have to make less every other thing that gets in the way of that, because every other thing is less than Christ.

Beginning in 2009, we would watch God begin a story that would radically reveal this truth.

15

THE PURPOSE OF THE LORD WILL STAND

O ur son Eli was born in 2007, and our son Zeke's birth was on the last night of our fall tour in November 2008. I left the show that night, went home, and we had a baby a few hours later. After Zeke was born, I knew I needed to get in shape to physically be able to keep up with these little boys who would soon be running around our house. Carrying around so much weight is tiring. I had to do something about it.

We had been watching the television show *The Biggest Loser* for some time. After watching a particularly emotional season, it seemed to us that I needed to go on that show. Kandice and I decided that the next time they were looking for contestants, I would go for it. It was about to be a new year, our family had increased, and the time seemed right for change.

Contestants had been going on the show in pairs. I called a friend of mine in Christian radio and approached him about trying to get on *The Biggest Loser* as my partner. Our connection would be two guys in Christian music, one an artist and the other in radio. My friend had already shown the effort needed by losing eighty pounds in 2008. As good as it sounded to me, my radio friend didn't think he could take that much time away. Plus, he had already lost a significant amount of weight, which would make it even tougher for him to compete.

I found another friend to try out with me. We made an audition video and packaged it to get the show's attention. Representatives from *The Biggest Loser* called back and said they were interested in us. We were exactly what they were looking for. That was affirming and a bummer at the same time. However, while they had a strong interest in us, they were only looking for blood relatives for the upcoming season. I told them I would ask my brother one more time, but that I was pretty sure what he would say. Jay emphatically said there was no way he would do it. He didn't want to be gone that long, and he certainly wasn't taking his clothes off in front of anyone.

With the chances for getting on *The Biggest Loser* fading, we began to look for other weight-loss options. Our team at the record label came up with an idea for a radio promotion around weight loss. Since my radio friend had lost eighty pounds in 2008, I thought I might be able to lose ninety pounds in 2009. The label team branded it as 90IN09.

The folks at Fervent Records talked to the people at K-LOVE, the largest Christian music radio network, about doing it with us. The K-LOVE people have always been big supporters of Big Daddy Weave. A friend at K-LOVE and I talked about what it could look like, and we ultimately decided to do a ninety-day event with them.

We asked listeners of K-LOVE to join me on this 90IN09 weight-loss journey. What happened next was a powerful revelation of how much people were hurting over this issue in their own lives. Over five thousand people signed up the first day. Over ten thousand people signed up within the first five days. Many of their stories were heart-wrenching.

Starting the process was an intentional and defining moment for me. I felt like there was something the Lord was going to do. In my heart I saw a redeeming year ahead. I saw the Lord moving me to action, and I was filled with hope.

Even though I had that vision for this journey, I have to confess that much of my hope was centered on wanting to look different. I hated the way I looked. I knew I was being shallow, but in my heart that was my desire. I did hope I would genuinely follow the Lord, but I also hoped I could change the way I looked to something I didn't hate.

Up to this point in my life, I had never known how to voice that self-hatred. It existed at a deeper level than I was conscious of and caused me to live and operate defensively. I would do things to protect myself without knowing why I was doing them. Self-deprecating humor formed the shield that became my main defense mechanism.

My first experience using humor to deflect other people was in Ms. Godfrey's fourth-grade class in my town of Gulf Breeze, Florida. We were asked to say what kind of dinosaur we would be based on the dinosaur's personality, its shape, or one of its physical attributes. I was in the back of the room and blurted out, "If I was a dinosaur, I would be a brontosaurus."

Every kid in the room cracked up. It was the first time people reacted that way to something I said that was intentionally meant to be funny. Their laughter gave me a feeling of victory. Even if they were laughing *at* me, I had a feeling of control because *I* had caused their laughter. It's sad to me now, but that was the most accepted I had ever felt up to that point in my life.

At the time I felt like I was controlling the situation. I wasn't someone's victim, because no one had said anything about me. But it was a reaction to hating myself. I thought, *I'm saying what you're already thinking. My saying it first disarms you, so now you're following me.* It would become a technique I would refine and expand in the years to come.

After I shared this story during the 90IN09 experience with my dear friend and counselor Al Andrews, Al had me write a letter to the little boy I was in the fourth grade. I was to give him advice based on my experience and share the truth I know now. I didn't think much of the exercise when I started, but soon teardrops were falling on what I was writing. Before long I was weeping.

Control is an illusion, but I can still find myself in situations where my anxiety has me thinking I desperately need to get it. I love to make people laugh, but I know the difference between the times when I'm using humor to deflect judgment I perceive other people making, whether they are or not, and the times when making people laugh comes from all of us enjoying something funny together.

When I try to gain control of a situation from a place of anxiety, the outcome pales in comparison to addressing that same situation in the authority of the Lord. When I consider the Lord's ultimate control, it shapes not only my actions but also my perception of what I want to control in the first place. "Many are the plans in the mind of a man, but it is the purpose of the LORD that will stand" (Proverbs 19:21 ESV). I can see things in their proper perspective and rest in Him, the source of all control and power because "in his hand is the life of every living thing and the breath of all mankind" (Job 12:10 ESV).

16

JOURNEY TO FREEDOM

December 23, 2008, is a consecrated date for me. It's the day I began the journey of 90IN09 with a visit to Dr. Asa Andrews. Asa practices a holistic approach to health and offered to treat me for free, which was a huge blessing. He issued me a challenge that day. He said that while I could wait and start getting healthy on January 1, 2009, why not start before dinner that night? I had no good answer for that, although there were lots of reasons I didn't want to.

When I came home that day, I began the eating plan for the first stage of treatment. It was very restrictive—no sugar, no artificial sweeteners, nothing refined, no grains, no cow dairy other than butter, no starchy fruits or vegetables, and no beans or lentils.

My body wigged out a bit in the beginning. A few times I thought I was going crazy. I talked to Asa and told him I felt like I was losing it. I had tons of anxiety and headaches. Asa said there was junk in my body that had to die. My body was used to living a certain way, and now I was telling it that it couldn't live like that anymore. Asa said that once I made it through that first stage, I would feel a lot better.

That was the truth. I did start feeling much better. The plan was for me to only eat non-inflammatory foods. I was also now eating everything organic that I could.

Next came exercise, and the new routine shocked my system. CBN, the Christian Broadcasting Network, brought cameras to the gym and filmed me rolling on the floor doing exercises for one of their shows. It was humiliating in a way, but I needed to be 100 percent real about this experience and stay committed to it.

I worked hard, and the weight began falling off. I lost about twenty-five pounds in the first couple of weeks. Everyone was like, "See?" More and more people began to take an interest in this journey. In addition to the thousands of people who had signed up to do the challenge with me on the K-LOVE website, K-LOVE was getting calls about the 90IN09 challenge all the time. The listeners were embracing what was happening and loved being a part of it. Dozens and dozens of people at shows would encourage me to keep it up, tell me about their progress, and give me positive feedback. I felt like Rocky. I knew we could do it. It just felt like we were all in this big parade getting it done together.

Another step in the process began by attending classes led by

Scott Reall. Scott is the founder of Restore Ministries at the YMCA and the author of the book *Journey to Freedom*. I went to as many classes with him as I could while still being on the road on a regular basis. That's where we began to get into the emotional aspects of the weight issue, unearthing layers of emotional stuff I didn't even know was inside me. I had never addressed why I acted and responded the way I did. I knew I wished I was like other people, but I didn't realize it was much deeper than that.

As we talked about the journey to freedom, Scott gave me an exercise using a sheet of paper showing what emotions were like when they are impaired. For instance, if a person has rage, that is an impairment brought on by fear. I began to ask myself questions about these impairments. Those questions helped me get to the bottom of some things. As I looked into my past, I didn't find the name-callers and teasers that I thought would be there. Instead, we unearthed that the criteria I was using to give myself permission to be okay with myself was how I thought other people perceived me. If I thought the people I was with liked me, then I would like me. If I perceived that they didn't like me, then I would be hard on myself.

Throughout my life I had been taught that how I should feel about myself should be grounded in the fact that Jesus loved me. I was living with His love near and having great moments of experiencing the love of God, but I realized that not being able to love myself was keeping the love of God at arm's length. I would thank Him and acknowledge that He is wonderful, but I was never able to accept myself the way He accepts me, despite His grace being enough to meet His requirement.

If through His grace I met His requirement, how could I not meet my own requirement? How could I have a higher standard than the Almighty's? Even to this day, I sometimes have to remember to embrace myself the way He does. I have to try and walk through the awkwardness I sometimes feel being around people.

Someone once told me that I was a very extroverted guy. I pushed back on that because I'm really not. I love people, especially people who are hurting, but I don't have the need to be the center of attention. I don't need to be around people every minute and be "on" all the time. For a long time I didn't know that it was okay for me to be like that. It's just who I am. I have to remind myself not to condemn myself for that.

Some people I highly respect were at an event that I attended. At first I couldn't figure out how to "be" there with them. I eventually realized it was okay to just be me. I didn't need to be somebody else. I was able to enjoy that experience, which was a sign of God's improvement in me. In the past when I've replayed social situations like that in my mind, I would think about what a doofus I must have looked like. Now I reflect and realize that it's not about me at all, none of it. That voice in my head just has to be told to be quiet and go away. It's still there sometimes and often tries to insert itself into my life.

The only thing that shuts that damaging message down is remembering the truth, knowing that whatever I lack in the natural world is not a problem for God—"For nothing will be impossible with God" (Luke 1:37 esv). All my failures, all my faults have been purchased by Him. Now I don't look at myself in a negative way all the time. I just thank God constantly for who He is. I don't hate on myself even when it's my inclination to do so. Since His grace is complete, I need to receive that grace and learn how to show it to everybody, including myself.

17

GOD BREAKS THROUGH

When we got past the initial excitement of 90IN09, the focus became getting to the goal. I needed to be self-sustaining on my eating program while we were on tour, so I purchased a little burner and all the ingredients so that while we were on the bus, Jay and I could cook what I was allowed to eat. It wasn't easy, but I was able to stick with it.

Midway through, I hit a plateau after having lost fifty pounds. I felt like I couldn't do it. Even though I had six months left, the newness had worn off and some of the diet wasn't going great. Lots of people were trying to help, but they didn't always know how.

Another thing that slowed down the weight loss that summer was our family's move to Mt. Juliet, Tennessee. I got out of my routine during that transition. In August I went to the Mt. Juliet YMCA and signed up to work with a trainer named Mikey Oaks. Mikey wasn't harsh; he was just firm. He'd let me bellyache about everything, but at the end of a complaining session, I still had to do twenty reps of this, twenty more reps of that. He became an awesome friend. I learned new things all the time in my sessions with Mikey—from helpful information related to weight loss to new insight about myself. Mikey would demand things of me that in my mind I was sure I couldn't do. But when it got down to it, I could do them. I couldn't believe it. The workouts became addicting.

Mikey would take me into the room used for group classes after people had left. He had me sweating over every inch of that wood floor. I called it the Flapatorium. I jumped rope all over that thing. I crawled, rolled, and did all the stuff I thank God no one ever got on camera. The grueling training was awful, but at the same time I felt like I could do anything. I would start walking, then the walking would turn into an interval jog, then back to walking. I'd never done anything like that in my life. The touring schedule that fall was a little lighter, so I hit it hard. Eventually I was down another thirty pounds.

I had one month to go and ten pounds to lose when Big Daddy Weave joined NewSong for their Christmas tour. After already having lost a lot of weight, it got harder for me to lose weight quickly. I was scraping and clawing.

I worked so hard every day. I would annoy hotel staff marching up and down the hotel stairs. At that point I was terrified. Fear and anxiety set in. I wanted to give everyone the happy ending to this story. I didn't want to let down all the people who had rallied behind me. It was almost like it was more for them than it was for me.

Every day I was desperately trying to reach my goal. When I was home, I would go into Mikey's office to step on the scale and check my weight. He would close the window blinds so I could take off my shirt. On the last day of 2009, we went into that office for the final weigh-in.

I had gotten on the treadmill earlier that day and walked ten miles. My feet almost fell off. I wanted to do everything I could before I stood on that scale. I was still in the 270s, so it wasn't like I was tiny. I told myself that it didn't really matter. I had done great either way. Everything that happened over this year was no small thing.

I got on the scale.

My total weight loss for 2009 was eighty-four pounds.

I heard something in Mikey's voice say it was okay, that we'd lose the rest. But those six pounds got into my heart. They got into my mind. They began eating at me. No one ever told me I was a failure, but I also didn't hear anyone say they were proud of me. Looking back, I know they were first listening to hear how *I* was. They were being tentative with their responses to first see how I was with it. They could then determine how best to support me. That hesitation, though, sounded like disappointment to me.

I hated myself. I felt like a failure. It was just one more thing in a long line of "not quite," of "almost," another chapter in feeling like "the fat guy version" of a story.

That message started to gnaw at my insides. Mikey got a new job and no longer worked at the YMCA, but he'd come to my house for next to nothing to help me. Then I hurt my Achilles tendon. Meanwhile, family responsibilities were increasing and the schedule with Big Daddy Weave was getting busier again. Life was happening, but at the same time there was this thing rolling around in my heart. The flicker of hope had been squashed. The epic story of that year made it hard to imagine how the next year could compare. I had failed.

I wasn't seeing any additional weight come off. In fact, just the opposite happened. When I got injured, the weight started to come back. That injury then turned into something else that hurt. As momentum died, it became easier to let go and not stay in the fight. With every bit of motivation that faded, a pound came back on in self-condemnation. I hated every day.

Even worse, the concept I'd discovered in *Journey to Freedom* about how I'd been giving myself permission to like myself based on my perception of how other people felt about me became an even simpler, more stark realization. It dawned on me that *I* didn't like me. *I* wasn't okay with me. When that revelation occurred, I felt like I had punched myself in the face. It was such an odd thing to discover. When I realized I didn't like myself, I went off the deep end. I didn't know what to do with that information. I knew that God truly loved me, but I also knew I was really screwed up. My first reaction was not to think about it, but that stuff can't be put off forever.

Sometimes I would walk around and replay parts of my life I was embarrassed about. I didn't know how to talk about it, so I kept turning it over in my mind again and again. I was wandering around trying to get away from it. Food is great medication for that. Stuff that tastes good is awesome, so I just let go and ate, but I was also punishing myself. I put back on every pound I had lost, plus six more.

At that point I didn't know what to do. I felt like I would die if I ran into Asa Andrews or Scott Reall. I sat down with Mikey and told him how bad I felt about throwing away what he had invested in me. I said we might as well change the name of the group to Big Failure Weave. I was sick about it.

One day I went down to my garage, which was my man cave where I would exercise. I'd go down there because it was quiet and a place where I could talk with God, but now every time I went down there I would feel more embarrassed. I sat down on the edge of an exercise mat. I was wearing shorts with half my legs on the pad and the other half on the cold concrete.

I started talking out loud to God. I told Him how awful it felt trying to be an encouragement to other people while I was desperately starving for encouragement of any kind in my life. I hated myself, but I still knew that He loved me. I had never doubted that. There are very few "nevers" in my life, but I never have doubted the love of God.

Right then, there was a pause in this outpouring of pain. A peace came into the room. I became aware that God was with me. He said I needed to let Him tell me what He thought about me. In my heart I knew whatever I was about to hear was going to be life changing. I prepared myself for that, because I've heard God speak to me many times in my life—not out loud like the booming voice from the movie *The Ten Commandments*, but quiet in my heart. I listened.

Clearly, and in a still, small voice, He said, "I like the way you smile."
That was it.

It was like a tidal wave came over me. I started to weep. In my mind
I could see myself smile. Without anyone but the Lord there with me,
I gave myself the thumbs-up and said I did too. He began to flood me
with stuff He liked about me. He communicated not just that He loved
me but that He liked me, that He accepted and approved of me.

He told me it was because He made me and I was His, not because
of any attempts to live up to a standard. He bought me with His blood.
He went through the terrible event of the cross because He wanted me.

That destroyed me, bringing an emotional response that was overwhelming. Something was different. I called my dad right away. I was
weeping into the phone, not making any sense, saying that He liked
the way that I smile. My dad didn't understand and asked who I was
talking about. I told him it was God; God likes the way that I smile.
He knew exactly what I meant. I sat and cried with my dad on the
phone. Nothing was said. We just sat on the phone knowing that it
was going to be okay. If I didn't change a single thing about my life,
it was going to be okay. That was a game changer. I didn't make any
kind of resolution that day. I just said okay, I like me too.

In that moment, something got fixed. I'm not saying I thought I
would never hurt again, but something that was fundamentally wrong
at the bottom of me got fixed. And it was fixed by the love of God. God
broke through.

18

REDEEMED

That day the chorus for a song started rolling around in my brain. I wasn't really excited about the music part of it. It sounded too plain to me. The rhymes were sort of trite to me as well, but it stayed with me.

During this time, Big Daddy Weave was recording a new album that was an uphill battle in every way. During our first round of recording, we had agreed to try a different approach to making the album that our record label had suggested. That experiment ultimately became a complete creative and financial loss. After losing months of time and thousands of dollars of our album budget, we began recording again in the way we usually made records.

Big Daddy Weave guitarist Jeremy Redmon was back on board as producer. The producer is the person who guides the creative and technical process of making a record. Jeremy had produced every Big Daddy Weave record released after the first album.

All the work on this album was being done in the studio in Jeremy's house. After getting a good start and putting a great deal of work into the record, Jeremy's home was nearly destroyed in a devastating fire. Jeremy was now suffering through a terrible personal loss, and we were back to the beginning again.

Adding to the mountains in our way of making a record, Jeremy was also battling a chronic stomach illness that was taking a dangerous toll on his health. Meanwhile others of us were dealing with serious illnesses among our family members.

Near the time our daughter Naomi was born, Chad Segura from our record label sent us a song to consider called "The Only Name." I was annoyed to even listen to it because nothing I had received up to that point had been very interesting to me. Every song sounded the same. But when I heard "When I wake up in the land of glory," I knew I had found something fresh and needed to hear more.

The writer of that song was a worship leader in Buffalo, New York, named Benji Cowart. On his next trip to Nashville, Benji and I met for coffee to get to know each other. While talking about where we were with the Lord, it was like we were finishing each other's sentences. We decided to schedule a writing session together over Skype when he was back in Buffalo.

On the day of our Skype writing session, I was on piano, which

I really stink at playing. I began to play the chorus I had for the song that had been in my mind ever since my experience with the Lord. I played it for Benji mostly because I didn't have anything else to show him. He was massively excited about it, while I was only sort of into it. Benji makes what I call the stank face when he feels good about something. The stank face was happening at that moment.

We started talking, and I said it seemed like all I could see was the struggle. All I could see was the bad side, the problem, what was wrong in my life. Benji immediately told me to write that down. We talked about me being haunted by ghosts that lived in my past. Benji said, "That's a good one!" We were literally just talking, and the words were coming out. It just sort of happened. Then, before long, the song was done. For me, it was truly done—as in, it was now down on paper so I could move on to other things. We finished it in one session that went by pretty quickly. We joked that we hoped every writing session went that well.

I thought the song was okay. For me, it was like drawing a line that marked a moment in time or turning a page. I had expressed what happened that day in my garage and my experience with the Lord and would move on to the next thing. Benji and I didn't even really discuss that experience when we were writing the song. I was still a little too self-conscious to talk about it.

Benji took the song back to his church and started incorporating it into their worship services. He called me a few weeks later and asked if I had played it for anyone. At that point I hadn't. I asked him what he thought of it, and he told me I needed to start playing it.

Josh Bailey was our A&R person at Fervent Records. (A&R stands for artists and repertoire.) Josh was responsible for helping the artists in the record-making process and making sure that records got made. He had been on us to hear every song we had to record. We had turned him into a broken record, asking us over and over and over to send him our songs. He was just trying to do his job, and we were just being whatever we were being right then. For lack of a better description, it was a special case of procrastination on our part. I sent him the work tape for "Redeemed," and he immediately wrote back to say it was probably the strongest thing I'd ever sent him. I was caught so off guard that I was a little offended.

My dad is kind of my meter. He's usually right, so I sent the song to him. He told me the same thing, that it was one of the greatest things I'd ever written. We decided to test it by playing it live.

When we did, people began to shout things. They were rising to their feet and lifting their hands in the air. That had never been our kind of audience. It really took us by surprise. When we finished our album, we were leaning toward putting out the song "Jesus Move" as the first single to radio. We still loved that song, but people were responding to "Redeemed" so powerfully at shows, we felt like we needed to look at it more seriously as our next single to release to radio stations.

I called Andrea Kleid, the head of the radio promotion department at Fervent, and told her what was happening with "Redeemed." I suggested that maybe we should consider it for our next radio single instead of "Jesus Move." Her first reaction was shock from getting a call from me about radio single choices. It wasn't something I ever talked with her about. As we talked, she trusted what I was telling her and said, "Let's do it."

The Lord then proceeded to blow our minds. It was clear we hadn't previously understood the power of the message of redemption. The world is thirsty for it, and the people who receive it are transformed. Many people carry around backpacks of shame or guilt or secrets that are sometimes so heavy, you can see the physical effects of that weight on their bodies. When the backpacks fall off their shoulders and they give those burdens to the Lord, they become taller, stand straighter, reach up to the Lord, and are filled with His grace. They become new. "I have been crucified with Christ. It is no longer I who live, but Christ who lives in me. And the life I now live in the flesh I live by faith in the Son of God, who loved me and gave himself for me" (Galatians 2:20 ESV).

19

HIS POWER AT WORK

We began to see the Lord use "Redeemed" in powerful ways. We heard story after story of God using it to radically affect people's lives. We were performing in central Florida where a woman named Danielle came to the show. She shared that she had been through treatment for cancer. After treatment, the cancer went into remission. Sometime later she was told the cancer had returned and that she had developed a tumor. She couldn't handle going through it again—the fear, the chemo treatments, all of it. She was in a place of hopelessness. Danielle decided she would end her life.

Danielle drove to the beach, where she planned to commit suicide. While sitting in her car, she turned on the radio and heard our song

"Redeemed." It wasn't the message she wanted to hear at that point, so she changed the station. "Redeemed" was playing on that station as well. Danielle said she knew in that moment that God was telling her something.

We later heard that when Danielle went in to have her tumor removed, the doctors said they must have miscalculated something. The tumor was much smaller than they had expected. They made a small incision, removed the tumor, and Danielle was cancer-free.

In Nashville, Tennessee, a pastor's wife who began a ministry to women who were nightclub dancers forwarded a note to a friend of mine, who then sent that note to me. The pastor's wife and my friend had been counseling a girl together. They had explained to this girl that she was valuable and could come out of that lifestyle, that she didn't need to be treated like an object. The girl sent the pastor's wife a note that said at 4:00 a.m. on her way home from work, the Lord gave her a song. It was "Redeemed" by Big Daddy Weave. She said she pulled over and wept. She wrote that she was ready to come out of what she was doing and start a new chapter in her life.

We heard the story of a woman who was in the back of a police car being taken to jail. On the way she heard "Redeemed" on the police car radio. The next time the police officer saw her, she told him that night had changed her life. The officer replied, "Yeah, jail usually does that." She said, "No, no, no. The song that was playing in the police car on the way to jail by that Big Daddy Weave band, 'Redeemed.' It impacted me and changed everything about me."

The brother of "Redeemed" cowriter Benji Cowart is renowned photographer Jeremy Cowart. Jeremy related to us his experience of spending time in Africa with a former child soldier named Martin who was a personal escort to Joseph Kony and a top commander in his Lord's Resistance Army (LRA). The LRA was slaughtering the people in that region of Africa. Jeremy shared that this young man was forced to kill many people over the years in terrible, unspeakable ways. The boy finally found a way to escape.

While Jeremy was with him, Martin drew stories to illustrate his experiences. While he was drawing, Jeremy played his brother Benji's worship CD and the song "Redeemed." Martin hummed, tapped his feet, and sang along, as happy as he could be. Jeremy asked him if he understood the meaning of the lyrics. Martin replied, "Oh yes," while the song played the words, "I am redeemed. You set me free. So I'll shake off these heavy chains, wipe away every stain. Now I'm not who I used to be. I am redeemed."

A woman shared with us that she had been the prisoner of a man who locked her in his basement and horrifically abused her for about a year. The only thing the man let her have in that basement was a radio. On that radio she heard "Redeemed." She said God used the song to help her survive what was happening to her. After she was finally freed, and the man was convicted and jailed, she sent the man "Redeemed" in prison as a witness to him. I have yet to be able to tell this story without being brought to tears by God's work in creating such a beautiful spirit in this woman who endured so much.

What these stories prove to me is that God's love for us is intentional and unconditional. The love of God applied to our lives changes everything from the inside out. In the natural world we often want to see it the other way around. We can worry so much about the outside that we miss what's going on underneath the surface. Before the prophet Samuel anointed David as Israel's king, God reminded Samuel that although people value outward appearances, "the LORD looks at the heart" (1 Samuel 16:7).

God Himself looks inside each of us and calls out something that we didn't even know was there. We don't need to work hard at trying to *be* somebody. We just need to say yes when He tells us who we are and what He calls us to be. We say yes and believe what it is He says about us. His banner over us is love.

At the second K-LOVE Fan Awards, Switchfoot gave an amazing performance. Jon Foreman, their lead singer, climbed through the audience, walking on the tops of the seat backs. While he was doing that, he walked right over to where I was sitting. Later, I had the chance to talk with Jon. I told him I'd always loved Switchfoot's music and that when he climbed over me in the audience, I saw the love of God in his eyes. Jon started to tear up a bit and said that was the best thing he had heard all day.

I shared with Jon that sometimes I wonder if Jesus is angered by the things I do or the ways I fail Him. Jon said, "I know what you mean, but every time I think He's mad about something, I keep running into His love." After hearing Jon say that, I became an even bigger Switchfoot fan than I was before.

More importantly, he's right. God grants me His grace instead of anger. As I experience renewal in my life because of that grace, I'm not angry about the bad things that happened to me or the times I got hurt in life. The Lord brings healing—He takes what the enemy meant for harm and uses it for good (Genesis 50:20). The Lord has had me come out stronger on the other side. Even the memory doesn't hurt anymore. That's redemption. That's what only God can do.

20
BEAUTIFUL OFFERINGS

ven though we saw so many amazing things happen in people's
lives through God's use of "Redeemed," we also saw people who
were barely approaching what God is offering. Many said, "Thank
God, I'm redeemed," but then went right back into their same old
lives and patterns. Being redeemed is about more than forgiveness.
It's about more than the fact that our pasts are taken care of. Being
redeemed is a message of hope calling us out of where we used to
be and into a new place in Christ. It's as much about what we are
redeemed *to* as what we are redeemed *from*.

The Lord began to unpack this meaning of redemption in the
lives of the guys in Big Daddy Weave. The five of us could have had

the perception God was only using us when we played. God certainly could have designed it that way, but He showed us that every day is an opportunity to bless the heart of God through how we live. We can honor Him in everything we do, starting with the way we interact with our families, people we see in the grocery store, and everybody we meet in the course of a day.

This isn't us buckling down and trying to earn God's love by pleasing Him. It's a realization that because we are children of God, we can bless the heart of God by being subject to Him and directed by Him in every moment of our lives. The way we live our lives then becomes a beautiful offering to Him.

I experienced a huge personal transition, going from seeing myself as nothing and hating myself every day to realizing that because God loves me, today can be so much more than the same old way my life used to be. My natural inclination is to settle into my solitude and not deal with people. The Lord, however, has led me to be the first one to smile at a stranger or initiate a conversation with other people when I'm in stores or restaurants. That's a big step for me, not because I want to avoid loving others, but because I didn't think enough of myself in my old identity to do that.

We have no idea what God might be doing with our interactions with people, even in our casual back-and-forths with others. When we're interacting in the lives of the people we encounter, God's purposes don't have to make sense in the moment. We don't have to know the end result. We can just be avenues of God releasing His love into the environment of wherever we are.

It can happen in the smallest of exchanges. God can do the miraculous through a smile, a "good morning," or cutting up with someone. The situation might not seem significant to us, but it might be the moment that person needs. It might be a moment of hope to get them to the next place where they might have a life-changing experience with God. If we aren't willing to believe that God can do that with us, then we're missing opportunities. We'll just go back into ourselves, so into our own agendas that we'll miss seeing our interactions in life as opportunities.

A story was shared with us by a person who was in Walmart to buy motor oil. While walking down the aisle, he began singing our song "Redeemed." As he continued singing, he heard someone a couple of aisles over begin singing "Redeemed" right along with him! Then a third man came around the corner and asked him, "What do you mean when you sing you are redeemed?"

The person sharing this with us said he looked up and thought, *Really, Lord, right here in the oil aisle at Walmart?* He then began to get teary-eyed when he thought about the man never having had the opportunity to hear about the Lord. He pulled out the only Bible he had, the one on his cell phone, and began to tell the man what being redeemed meant.

Meanwhile, the other man a couple of aisles over who had been singing "Redeemed" with him came around and asked if he could join them. He said, "Absolutely! C'mon!" He went on to tell the man who asked the question about how Christ came to this earth with the sole purpose of dying on a cross for each of them and for everyone. He told the man how Jesus lived a sinless life and was the one and only perfect sacrifice for us. He explained that the story didn't stop there. The death of Christ meant nothing until He rose from the grave. He told the man that he served a risen Savior.

Right there in front of the 10W-30 oil cans, the man telling the story, the person who sang along with him, and the stranger who asked the question knelt together. The man who asked the question gave his life to Christ. The man telling the story never saw that man again, but he said he knows one day he will see him in heaven.

Who knows except the Lord how many other interactions there were that led up to the man asking that question about the meaning of being redeemed. For the teller of the story, it would have been easy to dismiss the question from the stranger and find some reason to move along. He, however, took a simple interaction and acted upon it to affect another person's life for eternity. Now people reading this story will be affected by it with the results being something we can only imagine. What a God!

We've been redeemed to be beautiful offerings, and we're given a sense of purpose like we've never had before. We are here on earth to contend for the heart of God. I felt like I skipped over that for so long. As many times as I've said the Lord's Prayer, I only recently realized I had missed out on His heart in it. When the disciples asked Jesus how to pray, He told them, "Father in heaven, holy is Your name. *Your kingdom come.* Your will be done, *here on earth* like it is in heaven" (Matthew 6:9–10, my paraphrase).

During Jesus' time on earth, He talked about the kingdom of God everywhere He went. When I realized that, verses about the kingdom of God began to jump off the pages of the Bible at me. The kingdom of God is within you, He says. The kingdom of heaven is at hand. The kingdom of heaven is righteousness, peace, and joy in the Holy Spirit. He would say these things and then put those truths on display. The leper came to Him and said, "Lord, if you are willing, you can make me clean." Jesus replied, "I am willing" (Luke 5:12–13). The leper was beyond believing. He *knew* the power of the kingdom of God and had the expectation that he could see it on earth as it is in heaven.

I settled for less for a long time because I didn't always get immediate answers. I'd try something and when I didn't see a result right away, I'd give up. When does that approach ever get results? If you want muscles, you're going to have to exercise for quite some time before the results appear. If you want sunshine, sometimes you're going to have to hang in there through the clouds and the rain. In the same way, there's a hanging in there while waiting for God's will to "be done, on earth as it is in heaven" (Matthew 6:10). When Jesus was born, the angels sang about gifts being given to humanity at that very moment: "Glory to God in the highest, and on earth peace, goodwill toward men!" (Luke 2:14 NKJV). Sometimes we receive these gifts of peace and goodwill now; sometimes we need to wait for them. They are revealed in God's own time.

When Jesus said, "As it is in heaven," (Matthew 6:10), He was instructing us on how we're supposed to ask God for things. We are to subject our entire selves to Him and look eagerly for His kingdom to come. Yes, we will still see hurt in people's lives. When we do, we'll hurt with them. We may suffer, too, but this is a new and different life He's given us. Living as beautiful offerings, we live in daily expectation of seeing His kingdom come.

21

ACTING ON FAITH

When I was still in college, Russ Lee, who had a been a member of the Christian music groups Truth and NewSong, was performing as a solo artist. He would later return to NewSong, but at that time Russ invited Big Daddy Weave to back him up for a few events. We would play his songs for him, and then he would give us a spot in the middle of his set to play Big Daddy Weave songs. Around that same point in the evening, Russ would talk about the opportunity of child sponsorship.

In the afternoon before a show, Russ and his family would set packets on the seats in the auditorium containing the photos of children who could be sponsored. I had grown up knowing that my parents sponsored kids, so I was familiar with the concept. When Russ gave an invitation that night for people to become child sponsors, I was deeply moved. His description of the work being done by regular people like us through World Vision stuck in my mind. I knew sponsoring a child would be something I would do at some point. To me, this work reflected these words of Jesus:

"'For I was hungry and you gave me something to eat, I was thirsty and you gave me something to drink, I was a stranger and you invited me in, I needed clothes and you clothed me, I was sick and you looked after me, I was in prison and you came to visit me.'

"Then the righteous will answer him, 'Lord, when did we see you hungry and feed you, or thirsty and give you something to drink? When did we see you a stranger and invite you in, or needing clothes and clothe you? When did we see you sick or in prison and go to visit you?'

"The King will reply, 'Truly I tell you, whatever you did for one of the least of these brothers and sisters of mine, you did for me.'" (Matthew 25:35–40)

Some years later, Big Daddy Weave began partnering with World Vision on our own tours. Our experiences with World Vision were very meaningful to us. Hearing the stories of how children all over the world were being helped compelled Kandice and me to sponsor our first child. During our What I Was Made For tour in the fall of

2005, we sponsored a little boy from Tanzania named Babayetu. I was instantly in love with him just because of his cool name.

During our concert tours, the folks from World Vision would tell me, "We would love to take you on a trip at some point to see firsthand the work being done through child sponsorship." My reply would be, "That's awesome. I'm not really interested in that, but I'm so glad about what y'all are doing." I shared with them my experiences with Russ Lee and told them how much I believed in it. I just wasn't interested in traveling somewhere else in the world.

That next year we joined with Mark Schultz on the Broken and Beautiful Tour. Mark's team had engaged World Vision to become a sponsor of the tour concerts. Our manager called me and said the tour needed someone to give a talk during a break in the concert about the opportunity to sponsor children. They were asking if I would do it. Our tours had been presented by World Vision, but I had never done anything like this before.

I remember thinking how odd it would be for people to see a big fat guy sharing about starving children. The picture of that in my mind just didn't make sense. I thought to myself, *World Vision needs to find somebody who looks a little more starving to share about this.* It seemed like it would be awkward because of how I saw myself and my own insecurities. I was scared about it, but I said I'd do it.

World Vision gave me a lot of facts to share, and I tried sharing them with audiences, but I never felt like we connected with people doing that. We had to somehow share from the heart. Since I had never been on a trip with World Vision, I had a very limited view of their work. Still, I knew whenever I heard stories about people hurting because of where they lived in the world, my heart would always break over that.

To bring heart to the appeal, I began using humor when sharing with people at the shows. I told them how I thought it was strange for a big guy to be on stage talking about starving children. I would joke with audiences that I knew what they were thinking: "I know you've got some Twinkies stashed around here somewhere, big fella. Why don't you give up some of those for the starving children?" It always got a laugh. It would bring down the wall people naturally put up when they feel like they're being asked to do something. When people laugh and relax, it allows them to hear. That became our entrance into real sharing about child sponsorship.

The Big Daddy Weave guys and I finally got to see World Vision's work firsthand in 2008 in Ecuador. It was an incredible experience. We met the most amazing people, some of whom had even been sponsored children themselves. They were helping communities with everything from working on clean water projects to providing food and programs for schools. We visited a school on top of a mountain sitting at an elevation of thirteen thousand feet; we were literally in the clouds when we arrived. Many children would walk two and a half hours one way just for the opportunity to attend this school. The experience impacted us deeply and convicted us to be eyewitnesses on behalf of the needs of these children.

My family had been involved in the life of our first sponsored child, Babayetu, since 2005. We would write letters to him, and he would write to us. We had come to think of him as part of our family. In 2012, World Vision invited the guys in Big Daddy Weave to go to Africa. We would visit Tanzania, where I would get to meet Babayetu in person.

I was nervous on the long plane ride to Africa thinking about what it was going to be like meeting him face-to-face. I would be meeting a real person, not looking at a picture of a child on my refrigerator. I knew we were doing a good thing, but there was something that still wasn't quite real about it. This would be an entirely new experience for me.

Once in Tanzania, we encountered so many sweet people and children. We met farmers who had learned irrigation techniques from World Vision that were helping them grow tall, beautiful green corn stalks out of what was once dry ground. At another place local women whose children had been part of World Vision programs sang and performed traditional dances accompanied by the beat of a drum. They had big smiles and laughed easily. I thought, *Man, there's just a joy here.* We were even able to record a group of Masai children at a World Vision project singing a part we had written just for them that appears on the recording of our song "Overwhelmed." The recording of the children's voices combined with the experiences we were having in Africa shaped what that song would mean to me. I wrote that song with Phil Wickham from a place of being overwhelmed by the goodness of God in my life. In Africa, I was overwhelmed encountering the goodness of God in the faces of the people we were meeting.

Our involvement with World Vision has provided us with some of the most eye-opening, life-changing experiences. We are humbled by the opportunities they give Big Daddy Weave to be a part of touching other people's lives with the goodness of God. Even though our goal throughout these experiences is to help other people, I always feel like I'm the one being helped. I was the one being blessed by the people we encountered in Africa. God was doing something powerful in my heart on this trip, but what happened next took me beyond anything I'd experienced before.

22

ALIGNING WITH THE HEART OF GOD

O n the day we were to meet Babayetu, we drove for hours. The last section of the trip had us turning off any real roads and driving across the landscape, being bounced and tossed around inside the Land Cruiser taking us to Babayetu. Finally, as we approached a clearing and saw mud huts built by the Masai people of this area, our guide said, "This is it."

I saw Babayetu through the windshield. My heart reacted, and all the nervousness went away. I loved him like he was my own child the moment I saw him with a love that was bigger than me. I was experiencing the love of God toward Babayetu.

Even though we had little in common, even though I didn't speak any of his language and he didn't speak any of mine, we looked at each other and smiled. I don't have any background in languages, but every place we've gone in the world, I've seen a smile and a laugh break any barrier. We may not understand each other, but each of us understands everything is going to be okay. We can have a mutual respect. We can like each other. We can get along. We can be together. We know that because we can smile and laugh together. We find a common place in our humanity just looking in each other's faces.

Babayetu doesn't have a whole lot as far as this world is concerned, but his family greeted and received us in such a special way. They rolled out their version of the red carpet, offering us the very best of what they had. On this hot day in Africa, they set out short, covered tables of food and refreshments for us. I didn't recognize what every-thing was, but in the middle of this desert-like place, I did recognize an orange soda. That really ministered to me! I didn't know an orange soda could do that, but they had gone to great effort to get that for us, and that meant a lot.

While I drank that orange soda, I noticed they also had a bowl of some type of cooked meat set out for us. I was told it was goat. Our World Vision representative from the United States traveling with us shared that when he and another person on the team visited the village a few days before we arrived, they had prepared goat for them.

In my mind, I heard, "They prepared *this* goat a few days ago." I thought, *I don't know if I want to eat something that's been sitting out for a few days waiting for us to arrive.* The people there were excited about it, though. Tiny children were reaching up onto the table and getting pieces of goat. It was a sign of how big this celebration was. For them to kill a goat was a big deal. That's something saved for a special occasion. I was deeply moved by the depth of their giving and graciousness. I felt my personal concept of generosity challenged seeing them give so generously out of what little they had. I felt so privileged to be partnered in any way in the lives of these kind people.

A member of Babayetu's family brought me a piece of goat. I tried a bite and found this particular piece of goat to be on the tough side. I chewed, chewed some more, and kept chewing, but it only felt like the meat was getting bigger in my mouth. I smiled and did the best "Mmm, that's good!" I could with a mouth full of goat. They continued bringing me more and more pieces of goat. I could tell they were looking at me thinking, *Here's this big guy—he's going to eat a lot of goat!* The pieces of goat kept coming. I had a napkin in my pocket. I would graciously receive the goat, then discreetly put each piece in that napkin. By the end of the meal, I had a pocket full of goat to empty out somewhere!

Later I found out that Jay had been in a similar situation. He's kind of a big guy, so they were bringing him lots of goat as well. Jay is not remotely adventurous when it comes to trying new foods. When they brought him pieces of goat, though, he would give them to the little kids, who were so excited about getting extra portions. He made some new best friends that way. That was so fast-thinking and sweet. Why didn't I think of that? Instead, I had a steaming pocket of goat getting nastier every second in the African heat!

Watching Babayetu and his family blew me away. I was taking part in a whole other life I hadn't really realized was there. I had never even thought about the people who live here before sponsoring Babayetu. Now I'm a part of their world. It was such a special feeling knowing that our lives were intertwined. Seeing these people who are truly my extended family showed me how acting in faith makes a difference in so many lives, including our own and the lives of others that we sometimes aren't even aware of or may never know about.

Babayetu and I started to connect on a deeper level while sitting with the translator flipping through pictures on my phone of my wife and little ones. I then gave Babayetu a backpack filled with gifts our family picked out for him. We all wanted to include something. It blessed me how serious and excited everyone in our family had been to get him and his family special things.

One of those items was a framed picture of our family. Babayetu held that picture and looked at it intently. He was really taking in the people in the photo. Out of all the things we brought him—coloring books, colored pencils, a jump rope, school items, and treats—he spent the most time looking at that picture. He then put everything back into the backpack and put it on his shoulders. He did not take it off for nearly the whole time we were there. It was almost like he was afraid his younger siblings were going to get it. He didn't know we had gifts for them too.

Babayetu gave us a tour of his family's home. Being nomadic herders, the Masai live in small, circular huts that are usually constructed by women in the tribe. They're made of poles buried in the ground with sticks woven between them and covered with a combination of mud, grass, ash, and cow dung. The cow dung is supposed to help keep the hut waterproof. Babayetu's hut and the few huts surrounding it made up their community of Masai.

We observed Babayetu interacting with the other kids who had come to this celebration. As they were running around and playing, I thought, *There's no difference between these kids and kids in America. They are so full of life and love to have a good time. It's like they could be our kids. They just live differently because of where they were born.*

While standing with the translator and watching the kids play, listening to them talk back and forth, it dawned on me that the kids were not calling Babayetu by his name. They were calling him this other name that to me sounded like "bunny face." It sounded like they were making fun of him. I asked the translator what that meant.

The translator explained that they were calling him by his Christian name. I was completely taken aback. What did she mean? She explained that because Babayetu was in the sponsorship program, he had the opportunity to hear about Jesus. At some point he made the decision to accept Jesus' invitation to be the Lord of his life. When he was baptized, he was given a new name—Boniface.

Boniface means "a better ending, a happier ending." I was blown away. In that moment, I knew that no matter how much I dislike the *traveling* part of travel, I would go to people who need help—no matter where they are in the world. I was convicted to share their stories everywhere the Big Daddy Weave guys and I would go.

That afternoon, Babayetu's family and the people in the village presented me with gifts of bracelets, necklaces, and a wooden walking stick similar to the ones carried by the Masai men. Instead of a bare limb of wood like those used for herding, every bit of the walking stick they gave me was covered in woven beads. It was beautiful. The walking stick beadwork represented hours of effort and care. We laughed together as they again overwhelmed me with their generosity.

When we first arrived, I was trying to talk and connect with people. The latter part of that day, though, I disappeared back into my mind. I was taking it all in and thinking about how powerful and important it is to be part of something like this. I was snapped out of those thoughts when I heard our trip leader announce, "All right. It's time to go."

We headed toward the Land Cruiser to load up to leave. Babayetu and I walked to the vehicle together, hand in hand. Our arms were swinging together. There were no words exchanged, but we were still interacting with each other, one person relating to another person. Even though we couldn't share simple thoughts via words, so much communication was still happening just holding hands, swinging our arms while walking together like I would with one of my kids.

As we arrived at the vehicle, the translator joined us as we prepared to say goodbye. Babayetu stood up very straight, like he was going to make an official statement. Tears were starting to form in his eyes. It was a picture of a boy working hard to appear like he was a strong man. I thought later how that can apply to all of us. At some point, deep down every person is still that little child trying to put on that they are a strong adult.

Then he said to me through the translator, "This has been a happy day. When are you going to come back and see me again?" I remember physically reacting like I'd been kicked in the stomach, realizing that I'll probably never come back.

I was thinking of what to say, fighting back tears of my own. I said, "I'm not sure when we're going to come back. We may never get to come back, but this has been a special day for me too." Then I shared with him, "But I promise you this: When I get back to America, back to my country, to my people, I will tell everyone who will listen to me about you and about the chance that every person in America has to be part of a special life like yours." We hugged. I climbed into the vehicle, and we drove away.

That day with Babayetu was an incredible, life-changing experience for me. I felt so grateful to be a part of his life and the life of his village. The opportunity to visit him was another lesson for me about aligning my heart with the heart of God.

I first saw that alignment in my parents. I saw it in how they lived, how they raised us, and in their support of ministries and sponsoring children. I saw it in my brother when he was just a child of about five years old. Jay would call kids who needed help "the Needeth." He had a jar he would put birthday money and other money in to give to those who needed help. Our family has always had a desire to give to people in need.

We didn't do that to make us feel better about ourselves. There is a feeling, however, that comes with doing the right thing. It's a peace that comes from being in rightness. Whenever we sponsored a child, there would be a point we would realize, "Oh, this payment is something we're going to have to make every month." There are often battles like that to overcome when we consider helping other people, but peace fills us when we give in to the right thing—even when the right thing is not necessarily what we would rather do.

The unknown can be scary. It's easy to be suspicious of people and situations we can't see firsthand. That fear can cause us to separate from the rest of the world. It can cause us to distance ourselves from people we've never met. Worst of all, it can keep us from acting in faith.

The mind-set of fear recalls Jesus' words: "Because you have seen me, you have believed; blessed are those who have not seen and yet have believed" (John 20:29). We're not asked to have so-called blind faith. The evidence is before us. As we have the writings of Jesus' life, we have witnesses today who share with us the needs of the world. The evidence is also within us as we align our hearts with God's heart. The Holy Spirit speaks to our hearts and inspires action.

When I saw Babayetu's face in the photo on that sponsorship packet back in 2005, I knew we were doing the right thing. That feeling came upon me the moment we sponsored him. At the time I didn't know anything about his life, what he did from day to day, or what the place where he lived looked like. When I visited him and saw the way his mom and dad looked at him, I felt the conviction of that peace of rightness I had when we first sponsored him. His parents didn't look at him any differently than I look at my kids. The world got smaller. Now I'm an eyewitness, sharing with others so that they can act on faith.

Jesus hasn't given up on any of us, so we shouldn't give up on one another. That's a big part of learning to live in grace. Just because we have some kind of difference—sometimes real, sometimes perceived—or just because we don't understand somebody else, that shouldn't keep us from getting close to each other. Those feelings clouded much of my early life. My perceptions of how others thought of me created the differences between us. But those perceptions didn't reflect reality. When we align our hearts with God's, we see the family He has invited us all to join.

Once I met Babayetu, I knew we really weren't so different. There's a lot more that's the same about him and me than there is different. After my experience with him and the Masai people, I asked myself, *What other places have I never even thought of where it would be just as delightful to meet the people there and experience where they live?* That's coming from me, someone who is indigenous to a highly air-conditioned environment within my little world! That's God's work in my heart. That's Him drawing my heart into alignment with His.

I have a vision of Babayetu sitting at my family's table someday, just like I sat at Babayetu's family's table. After first seeing that vision, the Lord showed me an even bigger picture: We're counting down to the time when the ones who belong to Him will sit around God's table. The petty things that bother us about other people are not going to remotely matter. Nobody's even going to bring those things up again as we sit as a family together gathered before our great Father. The closer we align our hearts with God's, the more we can take in of that heavenly gathering here and now.

23

THE BONDS
OF THIS WORLD

Around the time Big Daddy Weave signed with Fervent Records in 2001, Jay developed bumps on his skin. They began to appear in clusters all over his body. When he went to a doctor for tests, they measured his triglyceride levels. Less than 150 milligrams per deciliter would be considered normal. Anything in the range of 200 to 499 would be considered high. Jay's measured in the thousands.

The doctors were shocked. They ran the tests again, certain those numbers couldn't be accurate. The second test backed up the first one. It appeared Jay's body was pushing this unhealthy substance to just underneath the surface of his skin, perhaps as a defense mechanism, but no one could make a definitive diagnosis.

This began a cycle of doctor visits, more tests, and treatments that didn't help, made him feel bad, or made something else worse— or some combination of the three. Because his case was so unusual, students were brought in to look at him. People would examine Jay and speculate all kinds of diagnoses, but no one could come up with anything to help. Jay began to feel like a freak show.

These issues persisted in various degrees and manifestations for years. Then in the spring of 2015, Jay suddenly lost much of the vision in one eye. He found out that it had filled with blood. Not long after that, he developed an infection in his legs. At a summer 2015 show near St. Louis, Jay couldn't make it to sound check because the infection was so bad. I saw a place on his shin that was so infected, it had dug out a spot in his leg. I said, "Jay Dawg, what is happening? You have got to go see the doc." Jay called the doctor who was walking with him through all of this. She put him on a month of antibiotics. Treatments like this continued. It would seem like things were getting better, but only until they got worse.

At another time in a hotel room, Jay was shivering with terrible chills. The whole time under his blankets he was talking to Jesus about it. He was thanking the Lord, trusting Him, saying, "God, You've got to get me out of this somehow, and I trust You. I know this is not You."

Then the infection got in his feet and really began to hurt him. With his impaired vision and the nerve damage that was unknowingly happening, the infection was even more severe than he was aware. While we were on the road in November of 2015, following his doctor's instructions, Jay was soaking his feet in our hotel room. All of a sudden he noticed that one of his big toes had detached and was floating away in the water. He picked it up, leaned out of the tub, and showed it to me. It was one of the creepiest things I've ever seen. I was shocked and said, "What in the world? Is there some kind of protocol for disposing of a toe?" Jay Dawg being Jay Dawg, he just wrapped his foot, went to the venue, and played the entire show that night standing up.

That's an example of another thing about Jay. Besides the nerve damage and other things keeping Jay from knowing how bad things had gotten, he has a high tolerance for pain. When he was seven or eight years old, he leaned against a hot grill lid with the back of his upper arms. It burned off layers of that soft, sensitive skin. He barely even cried. By the time Jay would ever say something was wrong with him when he was a kid, we knew it must be something bad.

Not long after losing one toe, the big toe on the other foot fell off. We made it through the fall 2015 tour and into 2016 with the same cycle of Jay's condition seeming to get better, then worse, better, then worse again. By March of 2016, Jay needed daily bags of antibiotics and fluids to battle the infection. Jay, a guy who always said he was warm, was now often freezing with chills.

Jay wanted to be on tour and continued to play each night. We didn't hear him complain, but his condition reached a new low at the end of March 2016. At a show on our Beautiful Offerings Tour with Plumb and Jordan Feliz, Jay played the first half, then became physically unable to play the second half. He was lying on a concrete floor backstage, all of us gathered around him, praying. With Jay unable to play, we brought out acoustic guitars, sat on stools, and finished the night.

The same thing happened again over the next night or two. I told him, "Jay Dawg, you've got to go home, man." We didn't immediately know how we would finish our tour without him, as we had shows scheduled nearly every night, but we also knew we had to get Jay home. As we were leaving Fort Wayne, Indiana, on April 1 to travel to a show in Eden Prairie, Minnesota, Jeremy Redmon thought of Ben Blascoe. Ben had been the bass player for Citizen Way. We knew Ben well since Citizen Way had toured with us a few times. Ben had just recently left Citizen Way as he felt God was leading him in another direction.

Jeremy called Ben and said, "What are you doing, man? Could you come help us?" Ben replied, "Yep, I'll pack a bag." We only had to divert four miles out of our way on the drive to Eden Prairie to get him. We got off the exit, Ben got on, and he started learning songs right away on the way to the show. His presence ministered to me, and it was a blessing for him to get a paying opportunity in a time of transition for him.

That whole chain of events made me aware of a trend I was seeing. When God acts, when He blesses, there's often a multiplying effect to that blessing. It gets on everything, affecting multiple people and situations. That changed my perspective from asking, "Is this God?" to recognizing, "Hey, this is God. Look at all that this blessing touches." It's amazing to see how generous He is.

The day after the Eden Prairie tour date, we played in Fargo, North Dakota. The original plan was for Ben to play half the show so Jay could just play the other half. Jay's condition, however, was rapidly declining. If Jay was in the back of the bus, especially if he was changing bandages, the odor of infection and the smell of dying flesh would nearly overwhelm anyone entering the front door of the bus forty feet away.

That afternoon inside the venue, Jay was lying across a row of chair seats with people praying over him and hurting for how much pain he was enduring. There was no doubt about it. Jay needed to be seen by his doctor as quickly as possible. When we arrived in Bismarck the next day, Jay flew with our manager home to Florida.

As Jay began to receive additional treatment and meet new doctors who would try to help him at home, we continued the tour. Near the end of the tour in mid-May, I was on the morning radio show with our good friends at The Joy FM in Florida. They had arranged for a new artist to call in and share his testimony. This artist shared that he had been leading a mainstream rock band and was deep in an unhealthy lifestyle. While on tour in Spain, the driver of their vehicle was switching stations when he stopped on one that was playing our song "Redeemed." At that moment the artist said to himself, "I've got to change my life," which he did, and he became a worship leader in his home state of Arkansas. Zach Williams was now having success as a recording artist with his first single called "Chain Breaker."

Once again, I was blown away. It was a reminder to me that no matter what else is happening or how bad something may seem, God is working. He is everywhere. He is King over all. I don't have to be able to comprehend all that He's doing. How tiny would He be if I could? He does not owe me updates on His plans. His will for me is to live in His sovereignty. He says in the book of Isaiah:

> For my thoughts are not your thoughts, neither are your ways my ways, declares the LORD. For as the heavens are higher than the earth, so are my ways higher than your ways and my thoughts than your thoughts. For as the rain and the snow come down from heaven and do not return there but water the earth, making it bring forth and sprout, giving seed to the sower and bread to the eater, so shall my word be that goes out from my mouth; it shall not return to me empty, but it shall accomplish that which I purpose, and shall succeed in the thing for which I sent it. (Isaiah 55:8–11 ESV)

24

ALL YOU'RE EVER GOING TO NEED

At the end of the tour in late May of 2016, my family and I headed to Disney World for some time away. As far as we all knew, Jay was recovering at his home in west Florida. A couple of days before our family was to return home to Tennessee, I got a call from Jay's wife, Emily. I knew it was going to be bad when I saw her number. Emily is one of the quietest girls ever and would never randomly call. Emily broke down crying. "I don't know what to do. It's so bad. I can't get him to go to the doctor. He's in pain. He can hardly get out of the bed." I didn't even hear all the details. I just said, "We're on our way."

My family and I packed and headed straight for Jay and Emily's home. When we reached Jay's house and got out of our vehicle, my wife could smell it from the street—the smell of death, of dying, decaying, rotting flesh. The smell hit me when I stepped inside the house. It was overwhelming. When I saw Jay Dawg, he looked bad. The feeling of death, the smell of death, all of it was so awful. I was so scared I didn't know what to do. I was so overcome by it all that I couldn't hear the Lord.

A day or so later, Jay was going to get some X-rays taken of his foot. When we tried to help him out of bed and into a wheelchair, he cried out in agonizing pain. Because of his pain tolerance, that scared me to my absolute core. I thought to myself, *Jay may be about to die.* A friend, whose wife has MS, came over with another kind of chair to help get Jay to the hospital. But the pain was so severe he couldn't sit in that chair either. I was out of ideas, so I called the doctor and told her what was happening. She informed me that I needed to get professional help. Though it went against every grain in my person, because we were still believing that God was about to do something miraculous, I called an ambulance.

I was anxious, Jay was in agony, and we could all feel each other's fear. When I ended the call with 911, I heard as clear as day in my spirit, "Help is on the way." That sounds generic, but then the peace of God flooded me. The ambulance arrived. Being experienced health care professionals, the ambulance workers easily got Jay onto the stretcher.

Emily drove Jay's truck to the hospital while I rode shotgun in the ambulance. I was just praying to the Spirit asking for God to be with us. I was aware of God's presence, but I couldn't feel Him at all. We were on the way, hanging on, and I clearly heard the Lord ask me, "How does this stack up against your religion on paper?"

I told Him, "God, I know what I would tell anybody else in my position, but I've got nothing. All I've got is You, God." He immediately said, "I'm all you're ever going to need." That peace rode in the ambulance with us to the hospital.

In all things, I have nothing else, no other answer. All I have is His presence. I know that, yet sometimes it seems like I try to see how long I can make it without Him! Every now and then in life, I'll catch myself and say, "What is your damage? Are you trying to make a marathon of seeing how long you can do this without God?"

I go back to my favorite verses in Proverbs: Trust in the Lord with all your heart. Don't lean on your own thing. Know Him in your ways and He will make it better, He will make your path straight (3:5–6, my paraphrase). I've learned that lesson every day. Sometimes I ask myself, *What is wrong with me when I know that's true but don't lean on Him?*

We are often tempted to not turn to God. A little voice will whisper, "Hey, over here, over here, over here." But when you recognize that voice is not from God and turn instead to Him, you realize you don't need anything else.

Jay's doctor called us when we were on our way to the hospital. She told us, "The moment you get there, they're going to look at him and tell you they're going to take his leg off at the knee. Don't let them." And she was right; that's exactly what happened.

The look and smell of Jay's feet ran the nurse out of the room. I don't know how we could stand it. It was by the grace of God. It was like we had somehow gotten used to it, which is crazy. The medical team sprayed something on the wounds that acted like an instant defunkifier. I don't know what that stuff was, but I'm getting some and using it as deodorant. It was amazing.

Then another miracle happened. The stepmother of our former sound man of many years was the person overseeing the hospital. I had not even remembered she was there. She came down and made sure Jay was taken care of in every way possible. She got him the room that he needed, got him the right people he needed, everything. She knew the best of the best, and she gave him the best of the best.

Every single thing wasn't going exactly like what we wanted it to, but we saw God's hand in every bit of it. We saw His fingerprints on all of it, that He was straightening the path. Even in the sorrow of the bad news that we kept getting, He was there and living up to exactly what He told me in the ambulance. "I am all you're going to need. You think you need this outcome, but what you need is Me." He's my outcome, so I can always have hope.

We were hanging in there, but everything about it was just gnarly. My dad and I took turns in the hospital, but Emily was by Jay's side every minute. Years ago, when she had dumped him, my attitude was, "I'm done with you," and even after they got married there was still a hesitancy in my relationship with her. Now, seeing her sitting in the chair by his hospital bed staying and staying and staying through all the horrible things that were happening was beautiful, and I loved her.

I saw a redemption God gave even in that. I'm so proud of her.

Throughout this time when Jay's health was a constant battle, we had been on tour praying for healing for people. As we continued to press in for healing for Jay, we observed that stepping out in faith in God—contending for godly intervention, and even just sharing the supernatural love of God with people—opened us to be a target of the enemy. As my awareness of that grew, I found a pattern of the enemy attacking each of us where we were the weakest.

With Jay's health issues, I was hurting from a place still rooted in identity. While all this stuff was happening to him, we were saying, "God's going to break through." Even when Jay lost his toe, we were saying, "God is going to grow him another toe." We were living in that space and believing it would happen. We were seeing lots of breakthroughs in the lives of other people all over the place. It was beautiful, and we believed it would happen for Jay as well. Then when we didn't see that come for Jay Dawg, that hurt me in the place where my faith lives.

During the past few years, we had been learning that what was being provided for us in the Lord was the same fullness walked in by Jesus. Jesus was full of the Holy Spirit. We can be too. However, we can only walk in fullness to the degree that we are empty of everything else. You can't fill something that's already full of something else. When I didn't see a breakthrough come for Jay Dawg, the enemy took me to a familiar place of weakness for me and filled me with the thought, *If you had walked in fullness, your brother would have been healed.*

Now all of a sudden I felt it was my fault that this had happened to Jay Dawg. The thing about the enemy is there's often an element of truth in what he says. That's how he sells it. If someone came at you with a weapon, you would know you're under attack. When it's a suggestion, just a thought that enters your mind, it's much more insidious. You don't even identify it as an attack. Something might be true about it, but the enemy does not operate in the truth whatsoever. He's a twister, a conniver, a deceiver. That's what he does. Even though I had learned in this season that God is all I'm ever going to need, I bit on that lie and let it begin working on me.

25

GOLD REFINED BY FIRE

I wanted to be by Jay's side in the hospital as he faced a surgery that would likely determine his survival. Jay, however, insisted that Big Daddy Weave keep its commitment to perform on the K-LOVE Fan Awards kick-off concert Friday and the awards show Sunday night. Though I felt wrong about going, Jay wasn't telling us to go just for the people who were expecting us, but to go for him too. Jay sent us there, saying, "I can't do it, and you can't help me by being here.

I thought about those words in that moment. I was glad of who Jay is. Like all of us, he's not a guy who gets it right all the time, but I'm proud of his heart. I left with a deep heaviness.

In the initial moments of waking up in Nashville on Friday, June 3, 2016, the sunshine coming through my window, it seemed like a normal day. Then the thought hit me hard that I was separated from my brother who, as far as I knew, was dying in a hospital in Florida. All the uncertainty that had been swirling around us came rushing back—the angst, the fight, and the sense that we were in a war over Jay's life.

In sports or a contest, you can call for a break in the action. When you're in the middle of a battlefield, you don't get that option. This wasn't a game. This was a war in which I sensed the enemy trying to end Jay, to end me, to end everything. I felt that battle over my brother's life, and I felt that over the life of my faith. There was a voice speaking to me saying the circumstances before you mean that you can't believe what you've always believed.

On the ride from the Opryland Hotel to the Opry House for sound check, knowing that Jay was in surgery at that moment, I felt like a failure again. It was that old familiar feeling that has hidden just around the corner all my life ready to latch on to me. It's that taunting that makes me condemn myself because I know there's something better but I'm not walking in it. Then the song "Thy Will" by Hillary Scott and the Scott Family came on the radio, reminding me that His grace was already working. I knew He was in the middle of making our paths straight.

After sound check, we stayed at the Opry House, waiting for word about Jay's surgery. I was ready, braced for bad news, but I wasn't alone. Our crew and our manager were standing together, everybody holding up this huge boulder that was the heaviness of the situation. There was nothing good about what was happening, but I don't know if I ever would have known how much those guys are my brothers without that pain.

The news came. The doctors had to amputate one of Jay's feet. We were hurting so much for Jay, and we knew the battle wasn't over yet. Everybody was taking it hard as Jay Dawg is such an important person in the culture of Big Daddy Weave.

In the face of this news, we were going to have to sing the song "My Story" on the awards show Sunday night. On one of my calls with my parents, I told my dad, "How can we go out and sing this? This song is a song of triumph. Right now it just hurts." My dad replied, "You can go out there and sing it because Jason's story is not over. This is just part of it."

That night we performed at the awards show kick-off concert. It was tough with everything that had happened, but we also love the people we sing for and were committed to being there for them as well. When it came time to sing a newer song for us at the time, "The Lion and the Lamb," I forgot everybody else was there. I just knew that somehow singing that song was bridging the gap between where we were and where Jay Dawg was. I felt a closeness to him, like I was actually there with him. I knew the power of God was at work and supreme.

The power of a song is amazing to me. Singing the words of that song in that moment was like making the decision to stand on what that song says. Even if I didn't initially feel the emotion of the song, that declaration made the emotion come in line with the truth. I feel like it has something to do with when God speaks. God didn't build creation. He *spoke* creation. Because we are a new creation in Him, there is a power in us when we speak and sing, a resonance, a power in the words He gives us.

On Saturday I did an interview with Scott and Amy from K-LOVE. I had seen Scott the day before, just after we had received the update on Jay. Seeing him was a comfort to me. We had gotten to know each other through 90IN09. That familiarity helped me greatly in that moment. During the interview I shared the news of my brother's condition with the radio audience, many of whom were in Nashville for the awards events. People responded with such love and prayer. Everybody wanted healing for Jay.

On Sunday morning, June 5, 2016, we were backstage at the Grand Ole Opry House for the awards show run-through rehearsal. We got word that Jay had been taken into surgery again. The doctors had decided he needed his other foot removed in order to survive. It was crushing to us as we hurt for him. All of us in the band and crew experienced that terrible conflict of feeling happy that they were able to save his life while grieving the loss, pain, and trials Jay was experiencing.

After the lunch break, Ben Blascoe, who was continuing to fill in for Jay on bass, came back to the Opry House with his own personal tribute to Jay. Jay wears an Auburn jersey on stage every night. During the break Ben found an Auburn sticker at the Opry Mills mall next door and put it on the front of his bass. When I saw him, he was wearing the biggest, goofiest smile, and his bass had the Auburn sticker on it. I broke down sobbing.

That was an example of what I experienced that whole weekend. There are a lot of surface relationships in life, but people of all kinds responded to this struggle as though Jay were their brother too. You learn things about yourself when you experience deep pain. You also learn about other people. I can't think of another way I've come to know myself and others to that depth than in sharing each other's pain. It makes me realize the gold is worth digging for, worth seeking out and uncovering.

There's a heavy part of Revelation where the Lord is talking to the church in Laodicea. I identify with the Laodiceans because the words Jesus used to describe them also describe me in so many ways. The Lord said to them, "For you say, I am rich, I have prospered, and I need nothing, not realizing that you are wretched, pitiable, poor, blind, and naked. I counsel you to buy from me gold refined by fire, so that you may be rich, and white garments so that you may clothe yourself and the shame of your nakedness may not be seen" (3:17–18 ESV).

Those verses terrified me. I remember asking the Lord about them. The Holy Spirit said, "You're richer than you think." I then began to think about rough times I had been through, like when we lost our house, when I had my heart broken, and what was happening with Jay. In going through those things, even though they hurt at the time, God saw me through them so well. He sees us through to the other side, one way or another. Remembering that brought me so much peace.

I have often found myself hoping so much for specific outcomes, looking for a specific way for something to happen, and being so caught up in, "Man, if it doesn't look like this, or it doesn't feel like this, then it doesn't have value." That's not good. There is a truth Jesus revealed when someone called Him "good teacher." Jesus said to him, "Why do you call me good? No one is good except God alone" (Mark 10:18 ESV). Jesus was saying to them, "There's only one good, so if you're saying good, you're speaking about who I am."

When I consider that in comparison to a lot of other things that I put a "good" sticker on, some of which may actually do me more harm than good, I'm forced to step back and think about my choices. Jesus often shows up in things that feel like they are stealing your life and *brings* life in the middle of the pain. That's incredible. Only He can do that. It's natural for somebody to get hurt and become bitter, but it's supernatural when somebody reaps life after going through the gnarliest situations. That's something only God can do.

26

LOVE BINDS
ALL TOGETHER

The morning after the K-LOVE Fan Awards, I got on an airplane and headed to Florida to be with Jay. My family followed by car. More people started showing up in all kinds of ways—in person, through cards, by phone, or in preparing Jay's house for his return. Each in their own way was holding our hands through this ordeal.

We stayed for the next month while Jay was in the hospital. Jay Dawg wanted to go home so badly, but he wasn't well enough to leave. When he would get in a dark place, he would only respond to us in one-word answers. I would sit in that hospital room and feel the darkness. But then, just when we felt as though we couldn't take any more dark, God's presence would show up. I would think, *God, if You are here in the middle of this much dark, I know You're everywhere.*

We were feeling the valley of the shadow of death. Some days we would sense something almost worse than death when it seemed like Jay didn't know who he was. It shook us deeply since Jay had been the rock in our family.

My dad and I continued to switch out nighttime watch, but Emily was mostly the one with Jay at the hospital. She would only take breaks to come home and see the kids. Their youngest, two-and-a-half-year-old Nathan, wanted to know where Daddy was. Emily would try to explain it to him, but he couldn't quite comprehend it.

The day finally came when Jay's doctor said he could go home. We were so nervous. I had brought Jay's girls back to his house to hang up a "Welcome Home, Daddy" sign they had made. We put it up where Jay could see it when he came in the door. While he was in the hospital, a friend of Big Daddy Weave sent someone to Jay's home to clean the whole place and get rid of every ounce of bacteria that could cause infection. Jay's father-in-law had cleaned up their back room and put in a new shower with grab bars everywhere for Jay to be able to hold. It felt so clean and put together. Thanks to the love and efforts of so many people, it was almost like Jay Dawg was coming home to a new house.

When the day came for Jay to return home, his girls gave him lots of room as he entered the door. They didn't know what to expect.

Nathan was with Emily's parents. When Jay Dawg arrived and rolled in, he was so quiet. Someone rolled him around to each of the rooms. He looked and saw all that had been done and gave a quiet nod.

As Jay rolled back into the living room, the front door opened. Emily's parents had arrived with Nathan. Nathan saw Jay, but he didn't come running. He just looked. I'm sure he sensed the emotion filling the atmosphere. It was the first time he had seen his daddy in the house in a long time. Nathan eventually came over to Jay, climbed up on the chair with him, and melted into his daddy's chest. Jay wheeled into the other room and climbed onto an adjustable bed some people had gotten for him. Nathan climbed into the bed with him. Then the girls got on the bed, and within a few minutes, they were all laughing. I broke down and cried. Jay was really home.

Recovery was hard work every day for both Jay and Emily. They pushed themselves, learned, and did so much to help Jay's healing that summer. While Jay was physically improving over this time, another part of him was dying. Essentially being confined to his house was crushing his spirit. His heart's desire was always to be out doing ministry and touring. Jay has always loved every aspect of touring—from the gear, to the routing of where we play, to the everyday nuts and bolts of what it takes to be on tour. I felt like he needed to get back on the road.

In the fall of 2016, Jay was finally back on tour with us. There was a huge celebration among the band and crew. The first night he rolled onto the stage in his chair during our song "My Story," I lost it. It was a deeply emotional night for all of us. Jay began playing a few songs each night, then eventually worked his way back to playing through an entire concert by the end of that tour.

At the beginning of 2017, a new and long season started for Jay when he began to get fitted for prosthetics. Zach Williams, who had earlier shared his story with me on the radio about how our song "Redeemed" had impacted his life, was on tour with us. Everyone on tour tends to get a nickname. Our nickname for Zach was Wolfman. We'd throw out a big howl whenever we saw him. Jay had even gotten a shirt for him with a picture of a wolf with its head thrown back, baying at the moon. When Zach heard about Jay getting prosthetic feet, he went online to design and order Jay a custom pair of shoes. He had them made in Jay's much-loved Auburn blue and orange.

In all the darkness we'd come through and were still going through, the Lord showed us His love, His compassion, and His care. He often showed us those gifts through the people who blessed us. Many we knew, like parents, wives, children, siblings, family, and friends. Many more helped that we either barely knew or still don't know to this day. It was evident to us how many folks were not only called to help but also helping with an intentionality that revealed their commitment to the Lord.

The Lord taught me through those people that whatever the situation, even if I don't know anything else, I'm supposed to love. Just love people. "Therefore, as God's chosen people, holy and dearly loved, clothe yourselves with compassion, kindness, humility, gentleness and patience. . . . And over all these virtues put on love, which binds them all together in perfect unity" (Colossians 3:12, 14).

27

THE AUTHORITY OVER ALL

B y the spring of 2017, Jay was learning how to walk on his pros- thetic feet. It was slow going, with good days and bad days. I was still carrying around this weird funk that what he was going through was somehow my fault. I knew in my mind that was not right, but somehow my heart would not be convinced.

Earlier in the year, our record label president, Rod Riley, had asked us to play at a music industry event in Palm Springs, California. It would be during a day off in the middle of one of our tour runs in April 2017. We were honored he had asked us. He never asked us for much, so we tried to say yes when he did.

When we played the event, I shared the story behind our song

"Redeemed." I hadn't told that story in some time. The whole time I was sharing it, I was still feeling this pain, this guilt about Jay. The "Redeemed" story touched people deeply that night. These people had heard a lot of testimonies, so it surprised me how deeply it connected with them. Even with that encouragement, I was still hurting so much inside.

A lady named Diane, who worked for the association that was having us perform, had been very helpful all day, making sure we had everything we needed. Something shifted in Diane after we were done playing that night. She came over after the performance and planted herself right in front of me. Diane was a tiny woman who was now standing nearly on her toes. In my eyes, it looked like she had grown inches. Diane got right in my face and said, "What are you so afraid of?" My reply was, "Lady, if you had asked me this some time ago, I would have had a list of things for you. All I can think of right now is you!" She said, "No, I'm serious. What are you so afraid of?" Every time she said it, it seemed as if she grew in stature.

The fear in me made me want to get away, but Diane said it again, "What are you so afraid of?" I was barely holding myself together at that point. I replied, "I'm afraid that I'm not going to hear Him or do what He says right, and it's going to cost other people. That's what happened to my brother."

Diane replied, "Well, what does He say?" to which I replied, "What do you mean?" Diane asked again, "What does Jesus say to you about it?" It was almost like she was mad at me. I told her, "You're going to have to give me a second. Let me ask Him." I stopped right there in the lobby of the hotel and asked Jesus, "Jesus, what do You say?" With no hesitation, no holding back, He said, "You're perfect."

My first response was to argue passionately with Him. "No, no, Jesus, I know what I'm talking about." I was arguing with Jesus! I sided with the enemy at that moment and started pointing out reasons to Jesus why I wasn't perfect. He spoke to me once more, again as clear as a bell, "Michael, what you're having a problem with is called the gospel."

Look at me! I was doing it again, even after the conversation with the Lord that brought about the song "Redeemed." I said, "That can't be." I could just hear the Lord saying, "You're trying to tell Me again, right?" I didn't even have an answer for Him. He just stuck by what He said about me, even when I didn't. He told me I didn't have to figure it all out; I just had to know that He is all I'm ever going to need. As far as He's concerned, because of His blood, I'm perfect.

I knew I needed to agree with what Jesus was saying, but I was having a hard time receiving it. It caused me to examine my very foundation. I even asked myself, "Am I saved?" Through all of that, my heart was sure what Jesus had done for me was more than enough, but something needed to happen so that I could rest in what I know is true.

Not long after that, Jay's bus broke down while we were on tour. Since the next show was only a few hours away, Jay's family loaded into a Suburban. I volunteered to drive. While we were traveling, Jay got a phone call. I don't know what the news was about, but a cloud settled over him. It was like we were back in the hospital again, like some kind of entity came into the car and committed a bank robbery of joy. Some kind of dark presence settled over Jay, covering him.

I quietly drove to our destination. Once we arrived, I couldn't hold it in anymore. I confronted Jay and said, "I don't know what happened in the car back there, but you have got to talk to somebody. I don't think it's supposed to be any of us, but you have got to talk to somebody. Whatever this thing is, it's damaging to you and your family."

He snapped at me, saying, "Don't speak evil over my family. I know there's something. I'm asking God to deal with it." I said, "Well, God is, and I'm pretty sure He wants you to talk with somebody about it." Jay replied, "I don't want someone to shrink my head. I want somebody who hears Jesus. I'll talk to them."

In this season of life for Big Daddy Weave that began a few years ago, we've seen God do the miraculous. We are always encouraged when we hear other people's stories of God's work. Filmmaker Darren Wilson makes documentaries about what God is doing all over the world. One of his films we saw around that time was called *Holy Ghost Reborn*. There was a story in that film involving a ministry in Colorado called Operation Restored Warrior (ORW). Started by a retired Air Force chief master sergeant named Paul Lavelle, the organization helps restore the hearts and lives of soldiers dealing with the aftereffects of their experiences and the wounds to their spirits many encountered long before they entered the service. The film showed Paul walk a hardened soldier through his past while inviting Jesus to minister to him in those experiences. I could feel God turning that young man loose as we were watching. It was incredible.

Not long after that, we performed a concert near Colorado Springs, Colorado. A man came through the line to meet us after the show who looked familiar. As he came up to me, he told me that he had been so blessed by what he experienced that night. I asked him if we had met before. He replied, "No, I saw you play last year, but tonight I felt like I was supposed to meet you in person." I told him that he looked very familiar to me. When I asked him why that might be, he mentioned that he was a part of ORW. At that moment I didn't remember that was the name of the ministry I saw in the *Holy Ghost Reborn* film. When I got on the bus later, it hit me—*That's the guy I saw in the movie! That was Paul Lavelle!* Thankfully I had exchanged phone numbers with him at the show, prompting a curled eyebrow look from our tour manager, which told me he was about to pounce on me for doing that.

I sent Paul a text and asked, "Were you in *Holy Ghost Reborn*?" He replied yes. I couldn't believe I had just met someone connected to that movie. I told Paul this ministry was what Jay Dawg has been looking for. Paul replied that they would love to invite us to be their guests at one of their Drop Zones. Participants in an ORW Drop Zone spend five days with no cell phones and no contact with the outside world. The focus of those days is just getting in there and letting Jesus have everything. I knew this wasn't some quick fix that would make everything all better in five days, but something in me knew we had to go. It had the potential to be a defining moment for us. I was convicted this was a program that could help Jay Dawg. I called Jay and told him about meeting Paul. Jay Dawg had seen the movie, too, so he knew who I was talking about. "I will go," Jay Dawg said. "I will go there with you." I knew in my heart God was going to do something amazing through this.

Not long after that, we were headed to the Denver area for a show. I called Paul Lavelle to meet us. Paul came and brought along one of his buddies named Mark Patrick. Mark was a sort of Hell's Angel–looking dude but was actually the most tender person. Mark was an alumnus of ORW. He had battled alcoholism and drug addiction since his teen years before letting God take over his life. Mark had worked on the Alaska pipeline and in the construction business, but when he rededicated his life to the Lord, he asked the Lord for a talent. The Lord asked him what he wanted to be. Mark, who couldn't even draw a picture, said he wanted to be an artist. The Lord told him, "You are an artist." Mark began carving wood, and now he creates fantastic sculptures of angels and other figures cast in bronze. Mark's story was another sign of hope for us.

We made a plan for Jay and me to travel to Lake Tahoe, Nevada, in January 2018 to go through an Operation Restored Warrior Drop Zone. We needed to get to the core of what had been having power over us for a long time, some things for almost all our lives.

I didn't fully realize it at the time, but God was teaching me about authority. All kinds of things vie for authority over us. When Diane confronted me in that Palm Springs hotel lobby, the enemy was using fear to exert power over me, causing me to go so far as to argue with God. God showed me His authority in that encounter with Diane. He showed it to me again when He introduced me to Paul Lavelle.

The Lord is constantly working to move us closer to Him and under His almighty, all-knowing direction.

I love the account in Matthew 8 of the centurion, a Roman authority who came to Jesus asking Him to heal his servant. Even though Jesus offered to come with the centurion, the centurion told Jesus, "Only say the word, and my servant will be healed. For I too am a man under authority, with soldiers under me" (vv. 8–9 ESV). The centurion knew what authority was from personal experience. As a Roman officer, he was used to speaking commands and being obeyed. The centurion knew that with the authority Jesus possessed, He could merely say the word and it would be done. His servant would be healed.

I want that confidence in the knowledge of God's authority to drive every part of me. How great could my life be if I just relinquished all authority to the Lord all the time? There would still be hard times and challenges, but I know through His promises that He leads in love.

28

HOPE IN THIS LIFE

Big Daddy Weave drummer Brian Beihl and his wife, Kim, have hoped for, prayed for, and tried nearly everything possible to conceive and have a child for close to a decade. We have watched them pursue this with faith-filled hearts while continually experiencing heartbreaking disappointment. They have been on a roller coaster of a journey, believing and trusting in the Lord and then seeing things not happen. Their hopes would rise with each breakthrough, only to be dashed on the rocks every time.

We knew they were struggling, knew they were hurting, but after a while, a lot of us became unsure of what to say. Were we making it more painful by asking about it? People were trying to be sensitive about how to act around them, but we found out in one of our tour fellowship times that we had gone too far the other way.

When we're on tour, each afternoon after everything is set up for the show, the artists, crew, and everyone on the road gather for a fellowship time. It's a time to hear God's Word, a place to share anything anyone needs to say, and a time to pray together. We then pray over the audience seats. We pray that the Lord will be in those seats so that the people who come that night will literally be sitting in the lap of their Father.

Near the end of our Set Free Tour in November 2017, our tour fellowship time was just about to close. At the end of it, Brian, whom we call BB, stood up and said, "I've got to share some things with you. I am really hurting and have been for a while. You know that, but it's made some of you cautious to ask how I'm doing. Don't be that way. It's all right. You can talk to me about any of it. In fact, I want to tell you right here and now what I'm feeling.

"Honestly, there are a lot of times when I'm just kind of mad at God. I'm mad at Him because I thought this was the way we were being led. But if we were, then what in the world is going on? I may be hurting and mad, but I'm going to be okay. I know that God is going to work this out. I also know that doesn't mean He's necessarily going to do what I want Him to do. I don't understand a lot, and I've got so much emotion right now, but here I am."

It was beautiful. Nobody was upset with him. Nobody was disappointed in him. It was just the opposite. It gave us permission to check in with him and not feel like we were intruding into a private space. It was incredibly freeing.

On the next to last day of tour, we were wrapping up our fellowship time together. Our tour manager, Brad, had shared, and we thanked him for his message. We said thanks to BB for what he had shared the previous day, letting him know how powerful that was for all of us. As we were about to break to pray over the room, Brad asked, "Does anybody have anything else?" At that moment Jay's wife, Emily, slowly raised her hand. I immediately knew this was something big. I've never known Emily to want to talk in front of a group of people.

Emily began, "I'm where BB was. I'm there right now, and I feel like I'm dying. We're hurting. I can't believe all this has happened. I don't understand why all of this has happened. I don't know how to make it any better. I'm just really mad at God right now."

When she said that, something happened in the room. It was like *whoosh!*—an atmospheric shift. The transparency and the truth of it was powerful. It was encouraging and terrifying all at the same moment.

It's one thing for someone to be mad at God, but it's another level of courage and faith to *share* they're mad at God. The alternative is acting like you're not mad at God when you are, which is living an untruth. The stress of hiding that emotion, the pressure of living in that falsehood, is physically, mentally, and spiritually damaging. I know about that in my own life, so seeing Emily in that place, seeing BB go through what he was going through, and seeing Jay's struggle and not always being able to give voice to the hurt was painful. Seeing my brother in that place was as bad, if not worse, as seeing him lose both his feet.

Many of us are afraid to say when we're experiencing that depth of hurt or anger. Sometimes we're afraid of what others will think about us. At other times it feels like an attack on the foundation of our own belief. What we're feeling in that place can seem separated by a deep, wide gorge from these words: "The Lord is my helper; I will not be afraid. What can mere mortals do to me?" (Hebrews 13:6). Our fears and anxieties often create that gorge, and the enemy's lies help broaden the gap. Hiding the hurt and putting on a false brave face can reinforce the very thing that is hurting us.

The following day in the next town of our tour, I was at a hotel getting ready. Everyone else, including Kandice, was at the concert venue. Unexpectedly, Kandice called me. She said, "You need to get back here right now. Emily is with me. She's physically trembling and crying uncontrollably. Something's wrong with Jay. He's talking about ending his life. He's with Jeremy. It's falling apart here."

I hurried back to the venue and learned that the night before, Jay was furious with Emily for sharing what she was going through in fellowship time. He was hurting just as badly as she was. He was struggling with some of the same issues she was, but he didn't want to admit it to himself and certainly not to anybody else. He was trying to hold it together, but it was all starting to unravel. On top of that, he was now feeling humiliated that other people knew about it.

Jeremy had been one of the first to hear about what was happening and got in a room with Jay to talk. Meanwhile, Emily told Joe's wife, Amanda, that she was worried because Jay had a pistol on their bus. Amanda called Joe and told him where Emily thought he could find Jay's gun. On his way to meet Jay and Jeremy, Joe went on Jay's bus, found Jay's pistol, and moved it to a secure place.

Joe, Brian, and I went to the room where Jeremy and Jay were talking. I said to Jay, "You need to tell us what you said to Emily." He told us a fluffier version of what he said to her, like it wasn't a serious statement. I pressed him again. He went on to say, "Well, you know, maybe it's not worth me being here." I was completely taken back. I didn't know what to say; I didn't know what to do. At any other time we were faced with something like this, I would ask Jay to help me hear the Lord. Now Jay was the one who was hurting.

Out of frustration, I said out into the room, "I don't know what to do. Jesus, will You please help us right now?" I did not get the last word out of my mouth before my phone began ringing next to me on the couch where we were sitting. When I saw Paul Lavelle's name from Operation Restored Warrior pop up on the screen, I said, "Hang on, guys. I think this is Jesus on the phone," because I couldn't believe the timing of it could be anything else. I answered the phone. Paul said, "I'm here with our entire board from ORW. We just finished one of our events. We were praying for Jay because you guys are coming in January."

I told Paul that Jay was right there and put Paul on speaker. Paul continued, "We feel very strongly from the Lord that your brother is dealing with the spirit of suicide, that the spirit of suicide is speaking to your brother." I replied, "Well, brother, that is right on the nose."

When Jay heard that, he broke. He began weeping, sobbing deeply and heaving in his chair. We knew the Lord was intervening. The guys on the ORW board in Colorado began to minister to Jay over the phone. They began speaking life over him. They told him what he was feeling right then, and they were right. Many of them had been in that place.

Paul then talked to that suicidal spirit like a person, saying, "You have to take your hands off my brother. You have to close your mouth around my brother." Paul was dealing with that voice and that spirit in that moment. It was powerful. I was crying; everybody in the room was nodding confirmation around it, saying, "Yes, Lord," in affirmation to what was being prayed over Jay.

Later that day Paul connected Jay with people who could speak into his life daily. He did the same for Emily with a different group of people. The guys in Big Daddy Weave also made a plan to take turns checking in with Jay until it was time for Jay and me to go through our ORW Drop Zone just eight weeks later.

We began to know something in that moment. We discovered there was hope. Lots of things were still very broken, but something felt so much better because hope was on the horizon for my brother. That was a realization for me of how much power there is in hope.

For all the assuredness the Lord gives us in many things, He still asks us to hope. The psalmist wrote, "Behold, the eye of the LORD is on those who fear him, on those who hope in his steadfast love" (Psalm 33:18 ESV), and in Proverbs 13:12 (ESV) we are warned that "hope deferred makes the heart sick." When looking back at what was happening to Jay and what those of us around him were going through, we could still see the Lord's faithfulness. We may not have rejoiced all the time, but these words could not be truer or more encouraging: "We rejoice in our sufferings, knowing that suffering produces endurance, and endurance produces character, and character produces hope" (Romans 5:3–4 ESV).

29

HOPE FOR ETERNITY

We may not have spoken about it to him, but my dad knew something was wrong. At that same time he was dealing with serious
health issues of his own. He was having trouble breathing. He
also had a nagging cough with fluid coming up from his lungs. After
a progression of doctor visits, he was ultimately diagnosed with pulmonary fibrosis, a chronic, progressive lung disease. The disease causes
the air sac in the lungs to become scarred and rigid, making it difficult to breathe. It keeps oxygen from entering the bloodstream, which
manifests other symptoms.

My parents were both standing in belief for God's will in my dad's
health. They were praying and immersing themselves in Scripture

over it. During all this, they weren't really telling us the extent of what he was dealing with or sharing how bad his condition really was. I'm sure Dad was trying to protect us and not let it weigh us down.

I have since recognized this same quality in myself. I can be the guy who goes it alone too. But when we do that, other people lose the privilege of being part of our journey with us. I tend to isolate myself from people. I don't want to be that way, but it's something I find myself doing. The only way not to do it is to come out of isolation and reach out to people. When I do, those people generally know what's going on with me since I'm not only my dad's personality but also my mom's. And with Mom, you usually find out everything. It's a part of me I hope will grow.

I began to get a sense of how bad it was when Dad couldn't talk on the phone. Right in the middle of talking, he would just be quiet. He was always a quiet person, but not in the middle of a conversation. He simply couldn't respond anymore. As a result, our conversations would just end. There was nothing else to say because it was physically too difficult for him to speak. That was hard, as we were used to talking deeply with each other.

This was all happening during a very busy season for us. My dad was always such a verbal and prayerful supporter. Even at a time when he needed us home, he was still telling us, "Go, man, go. Go, go, go. Go get 'em." I have mixed feelings about that now. I'm so glad that's who he was, but I also regret not having that time with him.

In mid-December 2017, I got a call from my uncle. "Michael, you need to get to your parents' house." I told him we would be there in about a week and a half for Christmas. He replied, "I don't know if you can wait that long, Michael. I don't know if he's going to make it."

With that news, I flew to Florida to assess the situation. It was obvious to me Dad was having a rough time. I was glad we would be back again soon. My return flight the next day got canceled, so I ended up staying in Florida for two more days. It was a blessing to get that extra time with my parents.

Kandice and I celebrated Christmas with our children early so we could get back to Mom and Dad's house as soon as possible. When we arrived at my parents', I was in shock at how much Dad's health had declined in just a couple of weeks. As sick as he was, I believe he had been holding on for help to arrive for my mom. It was like he didn't want to mess up anybody's plans. I realized how strong he had been to stay alive that long.

Dad could barely leave his chair. My mom and dad have two recliners that sit next to each other in their living room. My mom had moved her chair next to his so that they were touching. She wanted to be right there with him every second. As my dad struggled to breathe, one of the only things that would give him a break and comfort him was when he would lean forward in his recliner and my mom would reach over and rub his back.

It had been more than a year since he had slept in a bed. He couldn't lay down flat, so my mom slept in her chair right there next to him. They were always together, my mom watching him like a hawk. She attended to every little thing, even though she was struggling with her own health issues. Mom has joint and spine problems that were causing her pain. It was incredible to see her taking care of him. My dad had done the same for her at other times during their forty-six years of marriage.

That's so beautiful to me that I can hardly talk about it without losing it. I want that in my marriage too. Seeing them love each other that way was a gift to me. They're who I come from. I'm so glad for that. As broken as I've been on the inside, problems with my parents were never a part of my story. My family has been a place of safety and strength for me my whole life.

In the middle of the night on Christmas Eve, Dad struggled to breathe. I got in front of him as he sat in his chair. He leaned forward and put his head on my chest. I rubbed his back and sang over him. I don't even remember exactly what I sang, but it would have been a praise song we would have sung when we were younger. Pictures of us singing those same songs in the car on family trips began to enter my mind. Those songs are forever for me. As I was singing this song over him, God came into our living room. The peace that arrived was unbelievable. I knew the Lord was with us.

After that peace of God came, Dad was able to rest, kind of, for a while. Since it was the middle of the night, I told my mom, "I'm gonna take a nap. If you need me, come and get me." Sometime later I woke up to the sun in the sky and my mom coming into the room saying, "Michael, I think he's gone. He's not breathing." She was panicked. I quickly went to our living room. The moment I saw him, I knew he was with the Lord.

To me, this wasn't even him anymore. His spirit was gone. Still, we called 911. I remember feeling annoyed as the dispatcher tried to help me assess the situation. I had already assessed the situation. The situation was that I was dealing with my dad's earth suit. My dad was already gone.

The dispatcher said she was going to have me try and resuscitate him. She had me get him on the floor and start chest compressions. I was compliant and did it, but I knew he was gone. There was a grace over that, though, as these were just the things that had to be done. When the ambulance arrived, the EMT team tried to resuscitate him and couldn't. All the while, I was telling them, "No, he's with the Lord."

That seemed weird coming out of my mouth, because I was talking to these people like everybody should just know that. Then again, it adds to the sense of purpose that not everybody *does* know that, even though it was so real to me. As I continued trying to explain that my dad was gone, the attendants put him in the ambulance and connected him to machines that were making him breathe. The doors closed, and the ambulance headed for the hospital.

Once we arrived, the staff put him in a room. Jay and Emily came to the hospital while Kandice kept our kids. It was Christmas morning. Our kids had been so excited, saying, "We're gonna see what Granny and Granddaddy got us. We're gonna have a party!" We had all these things planned, but now it was surreal. I have a sense of relief and a terrible pain about it all at the same time.

Our family doctor met us at the hospital. She has been like an angel to our family. She was always looking out for us. The group of us met with the on-call pulmonary doctor, who explained, "We can try to see where this goes over the next couple of days. Maybe something will take a turn." But he couldn't say what that really meant for Dad's brain. His brain had likely sustained some sort of damage since he had been without oxygen for so long. My reaction was, "Wouldn't it be better to take him off these machines?"

The doctor replied, "Yes, but we can hang in there. I'm not telling you it's all over, but I'm not—"

I broke in and said, "I really know and believe in my heart my dad's not in there. I really do believe he is with God."

The doctor, who had remained kind and professional throughout all of this, respected what we had to say.

And so we all gathered around my dad. I had recently written a song with my friend David Leonard called "All Things New" that had ministered to my dad. Dad had listened to a rough demo recording we made of it over and over and over again. I had the recording of that song on my phone. I began playing it and placed the phone on my dad's chest. We stood around him while the medical staff unplugged the machines. Very soon after that, the results verified everything we already knew. As difficult as it was, we began to let go.

My earliest memory of my dad is of him singing over me in the middle of the night when I was a little boy and couldn't sleep. I remember feeling the vibration of his voice as my head rested on his chest. My final memory with my dad is getting to sing over him. In that, I have the peace of God, a peace that my dad introduced me to. It was a beautiful thing—both beautiful and painful.

I thank the Lord for hope not only in this life but in the life to come. "If in Christ we have hope in this life only, we are of all people most to be pitied. . . . For as in Adam all die, so also in Christ shall all be made alive" (1 Corinthians 15:19, 22 ESV).

30

AT THE BOTTOM OF
THE OCEAN OF OURSELVES

In its own way, the passing of my dad was like the final preparation of our hearts for our experience with Operation Restored Warrior. There is so much soul searching that happens when you go through losing a parent. The loss of a parent puts you in a space of digging around in places you haven't wandered around in yourself for a long time. It's a significant turning point in life. This person you've lost links you all the way back to your beginning. I think it was God's grace that allowed us to endure the loss of our dad right before Jay and I left to go through an experience where we would look deep into our hearts.

After Dad's passing, we helped my mom get things in order around her house. My pain from missing my dad paled in comparison to the hurt my mom suffered. To this day I still don't know what to do with that feeling. As we were running around trying to help Mom, everything we touched reminded us of something we'd done with Dad or some moment in our lives together. As sad as these reminders made us feel, dealing with those memories and emotions helped to prepare us for how Jesus would work in our hearts.

The heavy sadness was like a sandbag carrying us to the bottom of the ocean of ourselves. It was weighing us down so that we would go to the very depths of who we are. Dealing with so much emotion allowed us to dig deep in our souls.

I was excited and scared at the same time to leave for Lake Tahoe and our time with ORW. My hope in going was for Jay. I was praying, "Lord, will You just heal this thing? Will You do a work in him to bring a healing that I don't even really know how to ask You for?" I didn't know how to ask because I didn't really know the depth of Jay's wounds.

The first thing we did when we arrived at the Reno airport was get our rental car and pick up another person who was a complete stranger to us. We came to learn he had been a member of SEAL Team 6. He had been through all kinds of stuff we couldn't imagine. Even after he was out of the military, he was contracted to work as security for operations in the Middle East.

On the drive to Reno with our new friend, Dave, we listened to the most terrible, amazing, and awesome stories I've ever heard.

About midway through the drive, we were asking ourselves, "Is this real?" When we looked at his face, we knew that it was. This guy did all the stuff they make movies about. At the same time we could see he was absolutely terrorized by the devil. We could feel it on him. He could hardly sit still. He may have been dealing with something different than what I was dealing with, but I've learned there all different kinds of brokenness.

We arrived at our destination in South Lake Tahoe and wandered out to the lake area. The place was owned by one of the ORW staff and alumni. We then met the other three soldiers who came to be part of this six-man Drop Zone. Everybody was awkward. We stood there and threw out phrases like "Hey, how's it going?" and "Okay, brother." Since everyone knew the ORW experience is about God, we were all trying to use our best church phrases. The people running ORW, however, are not remotely like that. They call each other brothers, but as a military reference, not a church reference.

They were also dropping f-bombs everywhere and laughing about the crazy and terrifying things that had happened to them. Jay and I felt like weenies hanging out with these dudes. We were thinking, *How in the world can we even sit at the same table with these guys? We're blown away by what they've been through and have so much respect for their service. They're like the real-life versions of Rambo to us, while we're guys who play guitars and sing about Jesus in churches.* We felt completely out of our league.

The Operation Restored Warrior folks, however, made all of us feel welcome. The multilevel house right on the lake was beautiful.

God's creation was everywhere. Having surrendered our cell phones when we arrived, we prepared for the next five days to interact only with each other and with Jesus.

The first couple of days they were telling us things I already knew. My heart sank a bit. I thought, *I could have taught this class and still be broken*. It was mainly informational kind of stuff, but it was good. It impacted me that they used a ton of movie clips to illustrate what they were teaching. One of the things Paul Lavelle shared was that story is the language of the human heart. That's why movies and other kinds of media have such an impact on us. They can climb over or around or under some of the walls we put up so that we can receive a message.

I love watching movies. As Paul said, they have the potential to be an incredible tool for sharing truth, so this instantly became the experience I liked most. At one point they played a scene from *The Two Towers*, a movie from one of my favorite film series *The Lord of the Rings*. When they did, I knew this was for me! Everything was wonderful. The meals were amazing, we were hanging out with these guys who were so cool, we were talking about Jesus, and I was getting to be a part of it. I loved the experience, and I loved being there.

On the third day the ORW staff said, "We're going to split up the group. Each participant will be assigned a counselor. The counselors have all prayed together, and we know who each of us is supposed to be paired with. Today is the day you're going to tell your story." Jay was paired with a counselor named Keith. Like Jay, Keith is one of the funniest individuals ever. It seemed like he and Jay should have been brothers. Keith is from Alabama, so he had a similar sensibility as Jay. It's another connection the Lord put together.

My counselor was Paul Lavelle, the founder of Operation Restored Warrior, the one we had met at the show. I felt so glad to have been paired with him. I already looked up to him, and we had a great rapport. It was finally time to get to the heart of our Drop Zone experience.

31

WHAT ONLY HE CAN DO

Paul and I sat together while I shared everything I could think of. Occasionally Paul would ask a question and then write in his notes. The first session must have taken three hours. After that, we broke for lunch. When you get dudes and good food together, there's a disarming thing that happens. It's like guys can receive something better when they are sharing a meal. We came back for the second part of the day. Paul came in with a list of stuff he had written down that he had been praying about.

Paul told me he thought I had made agreements with destructive things in my life. He said those agreements needed to be broken. We began to pray and break them, one by one. It was a long list of things. One of them was the word *disdain*. I could see it, how I had partnered with the idea of looking down on someone else for one reason or another, even if it seemed like a noble reason to me. Those types of agreements had created strongholds in my life.

The process was exhaustive. When we prayed, it was with language like a lawyer would use. It was very legal sounding, but that's what was happening. Paul was breaking off legal rights that darkness had in my life. We did that for a long time. I already knew I was in bad shape, but when we went through the pages of agreements that I had made, I realized I was more jacked up than I thought.

Each time we named one, I felt like I could see the time in my life when I had made that agreement. Some of the agreements Paul brought up weren't ones that I had shared with him. The Lord had just revealed them to him.

After we had broken all the agreements, we began to take a journey that was like a trip through my life. Paul started this part by asking, "As we look for the beginnings of the fear you have lived in during your life, did your mom have any reason she should have been afraid when she was pregnant with you?" I knew my mom had miscarried prior to becoming pregnant with me. That made her very concerned about losing me. She also had a bad fall during her pregnancy that had scared her. Paul said, "I think the fear you've lived in began in your mother's womb."

After that, Paul said, "I want you to close your eyes." For a second I had one eye cracked open a little. Then I thought, *All right, this is all straight up*, so I committed and kept both eyes closed. Then I started to see things in my mind's eye.

The first thing I saw was darkness. Then I saw a dark circle, which I'm assuming was my mom's womb. This next part is where the story starts to sound like I was in a drug-induced state, except that I've never done drugs. I saw train tracks begin on the sphere, like the train tracks on the old *Soul Train* television show. The sphere then turned into the earth, and then the tracks caught on fire. As crazy as that sounds, fear began to dissipate in me at that moment. It was like the Lord was addressing the fear. As I thought about my life and what I was seeing, it started to make sense to me. Traveling to places around our country and other parts of the world is what the members of Big Daddy Weave do all the time. God called me to that from the womb.

We continued going on the tracks. The first stop was a memory that had not been clear until this moment. I must have been four or five years old when we moved from Michigan to Florida. My uncle had just given me a new toy six-shooter with a holster. I was so proud of that thing.

A kid next door was a little older and would only come over when he was bored. I desperately wanted him to like me. It would have been so great to be accepted by someone older than me. I wanted him to like me so badly that I gave him that six-shooter.

He took it, which made my mom extremely mad. My dad told her, "He gave it to him, and you can't just take it back. You've got to let him do this."

The kid still didn't like me. In fact, he was always kind of mean to me. I knew now that was the moment I had received the idea that I was not likable and therefore I needed to try to get people to like me somehow. And even then people were still probably not going to like me.

Then Paul said, "Look around you now in that memory. Who do you see?" I looked, and I saw Jesus standing right beside me. Jesus had this huge Santa Claus–type bag. On the white fuzzy rim of the Santa Claus bag was written "Every Good Thing."

Then Jesus showed me another memory I had forgotten until that moment. I had gone over to that boy's house years later. When I did, I saw his room. His room didn't look like my room. He didn't have hardly anything in it except that six-shooter. He didn't have a mom and dad who gave him the things that my mom and dad gave me. He had to hang on to every little thing he had because he grew up without very much.

I saw a vision of me standing there with Jesus, the Son of God, the King of the universe, who had that giant bag with "Every Good Thing" written on it. I then went back to the time when I was four or five and gave that boy the six-shooter again. This time, I gave it to him not because I needed him to like me but because he didn't have anything. I did it because my heart wants people to have good things.

Jesus healed something in that moment.

Then it was time to go again. We started back on the tracks. Now I was a boy at a time when my body was changing. I was aware something was different about me. I was embarrassed by those feelings. It was like something was very wrong, and I couldn't tell anybody what it was. There wasn't anything wrong, but I had received the change occurring in me as a bad thing in my heart.

Paul asked me, "Where is Jesus in the place you are in this moment?" I looked, and Jesus was standing right there. I was becoming a man, and Jesus was celebrating the fact that He made me the way He had. At that moment Jesus took every stigma out of that moment when my body was changing that I had carried with me all my life.

Then I was on to the next part of the journey, to a time when I was probably eleven or twelve years old. Jay had come to me and said, "Mike, I found this magazine in the woods." It was a pornographic magazine. We knew one of our neighbors had been hiding it back among the trees. I said, "Oh, Jay, we can't have this," and I put it in the trash. But it pulled on me. I went back for the magazine. That began a struggle that was hidden in my life all through my teenage years and into my adult years.

I remember living in such shame about all of that. When I was in college, the internet arrived and became the temptation. Even after getting married, that kind of temptation came knocking. In the early days of Big Daddy Weave, I went to our band pastor, Pastor Jay, and told him all about it. He walked with me through the healing from that addiction, but there was still something about it remaining deep inside me.

In the session with Paul, Jesus took me back to that trash can. I could see in my mind's eye Jesus standing there when I went back for the magazine. Jesus wasn't mad or disappointed in me, but with a sober face, He reached out for the magazine. I gave it to Him. When He took it, He closed His eyes and then made it disappear. He didn't get up on the roof and shout that I had been doing something or accuse me in any way. He just made it disappear. That settled something in me. Something in me was healed.

The next stop on the train tracks was to South Carolina. We arrived on the day the girl I first liked brought out the book in which her parents underlined the description of why their daughter could never marry an overweight guy. I was standing there all over again, feeling like somebody had torn some of my guts out and left a big hole in me.

Jesus was there with me that day. I'd never seen that until now. He put His hand on my shoulder, and in an instant, I knew everything I know today about my family—how much my wife Kandice loves me, regardless of how messed up I may be at any given moment, and how much our kids love me. Suddenly the greatest relief came over me. Thank God things did not happen the way I wanted them to happen. I would have missed so much. Even the sting of the memory was overwhelmed by joy. I started thanking Jesus, "Jesus, thank You, thank You, Jesus, that You always have known so much better for me. Thank You, Jesus."

From there, in my mind's eye, we went to a clearing. The clearing was a big, circular field with old roots and dry, dead ground. Paul said, "This circle is your soul. See how big it is?" I replied that I did. Our eyes were closed, but I could see everything he was describing. I started to describe things to him and then he would finish the sentence, because we were seeing the exact same things. I was thinking to myself, *What the heck is going on?*

With our eyes still closed, Paul said, "I want you to see that circle like it's a clock. We're now turning it back in quadrants, going from twelve to nine. Just watch what happens." As it turned back, the clearing got green and lush and healthy. Paul said, "Now we're going from nine to six." The clearing grew and became more beautiful. Then we went from six to three, and finally three back to twelve. The grass came up so green. It looked like a piece of land that somebody had fertilized and taken care of. It was beautiful and good. When I looked back on this later, I thought of Psalm 23, "He restores my soul" (v. 3 ESV).

And then I saw a yellow road begin out of one side of the clearing. It led to this huge crystalline structure that looked like a giant hourglass. Paul said, "That is your spirit." My spirit was the bottom of the hourglass. The top part of the hourglass was the Holy Spirit. In the middle, just like a regular hourglass, was this connection. It was intact. The connection between my spirit and the Spirit of God wasn't broken. I'm pretty sure that's why we had been able to minister even while being broken. The Spirit was at work. Paul said, "This looks good." I'm like, *Great! Moving on!*

On the other side of the clearing, which was so gigantic that it went into the sky—was a red road that led to another structure. Paul said, "That thing over there is your heart." It was this great big old red house. There were two angels in front of the structure to guard my heart. We went into it. It was a huge and awesome house. In it were libraries of things, some of which were songs that would come from my heart.

This space that is my heart was beautiful and vast. Then Jesus came in and opened up the Santa Claus–like bag He'd been carrying with Him. It unfolded into the structure that we were in and filled my heart. I could still see the patch that said, "Every Good Thing." And then my heart was well. It was better. I can't say it any other way than that. It was like what had been very wrong was not wrong anymore.

Paul said, "We have one more stop." We went to my dad's grave. It dawned on me that's what the Santa Claus bag was about. Jesus was giving me back Christmas. Many angels were at Dad's grave. And there was Jesus. My dad was with Him, and they were friends. Paul said, "What do you want to tell your dad?" I told Dad how grateful I was, how I was so glad that he was my dad and that I was so glad he had been the one to introduce me to Jesus. I can't explain what happened, but it was one more thing fixed in my heart.

The entire journey was incredible. I've never experienced anything like it in my entire life. All I know is something grabbed hold of my guts that day and what was wrong was made right. It convicted me that there is a healing and a redemption for every person. No matter how ugly the brokenness is, Jesus is not constrained to time or events or anything else. Jesus can do a thing that only He can do, and He will heal even the most wounded heart. I believe there is that hope for every person. Name whatever has happened or whatever could happen, and I'm certain the hope of who Jesus is will be the answer for it. That's what I'm learning now as I see a lot of things I didn't see before.

After that time at the Operation Restored Warrior Drop Zone, things would happen that would try to convince me none of what happened to me was real. They were reflexes I'd become accustomed to in my life. I knew this was different. When I address things in Jesus, my wounds don't stick around. They're like dust that gets blown away. When I think about painful memories, it no longer hurts to talk about them because they are not even the same memories. The Lord changed each memory by showing me where He was in it. He showed me a new and right reality of what had been there all along. I was just seeing it for the first time.

This experience also removed all the shame from those memories. When I talk about a particular memory, it doesn't carry the same yuck it used to. When the shame is gone and the Lord takes away the fear, you realize that being able to talk about what you've been through carries the potential to touch somebody who is in the same yuck. "We know that for those who love God all things work together for good" (Romans 8:28 ESV). That's the point where everything bad that ever happened in your life becomes one more thing God can use.

32

THE ACORN IN US

At the beginning of this book, I mentioned that "Redeemed" had just won Song of the Year at the first K-LOVE Fan Awards. We were celebrating the victory in my life over feelings of self-hatred and not feeling good enough, celebrating the victory over not reliving things in my mind that I was disappointed about in myself. A week after that event, I was performing at a youth camp and began to wake up at night thinking how stupid I must have sounded giving the acceptance speech. It was happening again. It was as disheartening of a feeling as I've ever felt. To be back at square one just a week later left me with one of the most hopeless feelings in my life. I didn't know how I could ever get up in front of anybody again.

My family was with me at the camp. We had two rooms next to each other. One room was where I stayed with my family. The other I used as an office and a place to concentrate. I sat in that room and thought. Every time I would go in there, the feelings of embarrassment about my acceptance speech would hit me again. I called in to K-LOVE that week and talked with them on the air, thanking all the people who were part of it. I was truly thankful and happy for what had happened, but then I would come back to that room completely disappointed in myself and disappointed that the self-hating was back. The two disappointments would then compound on each other. It was terrible.

I was sitting in that room when someone sent me a text message that they had seen a video of the acceptance speech on Kandice's Facebook page. I went crazy. I got mad and texted Kandice, asking her why she would do something like that. I was so embarrassed, thinking in my mind that it must have been horrible. I hadn't seen it, but I was listening to the liar who was talking to me.

As I finished the text, the Holy Spirit told me to watch the video. That made me mad at the Lord. I couldn't understand why He would want me to see that. I was defending the self-hatred! He said, "Just watch it." The page for the video was sitting there in front of me on my screen. I stared at it for a while before finally pressing play. This is what I had said:

The truth is, man, before we came here tonight, my little boy, Eli, who fell asleep before the awards got started good, he was gonna listen on the app online. He said, "Daddy, I'm nervous." I said, "Don't be nervous, baby, 'cause the truth is, we already won." Amen? And that's what we win, is Him. Man, I hated my own guts for so long. There's nothing worse than being a guy who's supposed to get up and encourage other people and hating your own guts. But I don't hate myself anymore because Jesus showed me who I am. We need to learn to see ourselves the way Jesus sees us, and that's covered in His precious blood.

That was it. There wasn't one thing wrong with it. Even so, the liar started again. It was like the devil was trying to take my lunch money one more time, and I was letting him. I couldn't believe it. With all I had been through, I was trying to go back to a place of shame and self-hatred.

Then I heard something like the sound of screeching brakes. The Lord said, "What you just processed in a week used to take months to sort through." I was close to having that victory stolen from me, but He wouldn't allow it.

Sometime later I heard a message that said religion only celebrates perfection but God celebrates progress. It made me realize that we are constantly in a state of learning and growing. My dealing again with something I thought had been beaten doesn't discount all the previous victories. It's like something our manager observed and shared with us, that the road to perfection and the road to spiritual fulfillment in the Lord are two parallel paths that sometimes look similar. The difference is, the path to perfection leads to disappointment, despair, and depression. The path toward spiritual fulfillment leads to our Father, who is perfect for us, and we are perfect in Him.

In the early years of Big Daddy Weave, we were shocked when our drummer, Jeff Jones, announced he was going to try surfing. Surfing wasn't something we ever would have expected him to do. Jeff had a friend who was getting pretty good at it. We were near this friend and the beach at the time, so Jeff went to give it a try. When he got back, Jeff told us about getting on the surfboard and paddling out with his friend. When the first wave came, Jeff was caught and tossed off his board into the ocean. He said he was terrified for his life, screaming for help. His friend yelled two words to him: "Stand up!" Jeff was in water shallow enough to stand in but he didn't know it.

Those words apply to my life every day. When I encounter traps the enemy has for me and remember who I am in Jesus, I'm no longer trapped. As quickly as that oppression came upon me after watching the acceptance speech, it went away just as fast. The Lord was telling me to stand up. Stand up in who I am in Him. My natural perception of my identity is based on what I think I'm doing well and what I don't think I'm doing very well. The enemy uses and magnifies those thoughts to distort my perception of who I am. The truth is, it's the Lord who says who I am.

David said, "Magnify the LORD with me" (Psalm 34:3 ESV). It's not that we make God bigger, but we see Him rightly. He is supreme. There's no one bigger than the Lord. No one supersedes Him. When we see Him rightly, we also see who we are. We are His, washed clean in His blood. When we do that, we're not so easily tricked anymore.

I was invited to an event for worship leaders called Gather at Bethel Church in California. I went and was like a kid in a candy store in one way and a middle schooler getting beat up by high school bullies in another way. I loved it because I love and respect all the leaders from the global worship community so much, but I felt insecure on the inside because I didn't feel like I deserved to be among them. The enemy was having a heyday with me.

Some of the people attending the event were worship leaders I had known about for years, like Don Potter, Leonard Jones, and Suzy Wills. I've been familiar with them since I was in high school. They were wide-eyed, too, taking in the people who were there but also seeing how much this community had grown. I could tell by looking at these early generation worship leaders that they were beat up. They had been through a lot, especially in the early years when they were introducing the worship music we know now, taking licks and never seeing the reward a lot of us have seen.

Kari Jobe, who was also ministered to by these same folks in her early days, shared a word with them. The Holy Spirit told her to google how long it takes for an oak tree to grow. She did and shared with everyone that it takes twenty years for an acorn to grow into a fully mature oak tree. Kari addressed these groundbreaking worship leaders, saying, "If you've ever wondered where the tree is from the seed planted in you, look around this room." Nearly every major worship leader in the world was present. Those people who were there in the beginning of worship leading, at a time when there wasn't much acceptance for it, were moved to tears in the power of that revelation.

I was so blessed by that. It applies to me as I look at my life. When I feel like I'm still struggling in some of the same old ways, I know I'm really not because *I* am not the same. I'm a new, redeemed person growing in God, and God is the One who decided that it would take twenty years for an oak tree to grow. When He looked at the oak tree, He said, "It's good." He is the One who makes things the way they are, in His time and by His design.

God is a lifer with us. He's in for the whole thing. That's His idea. We don't have to get it all nailed down today. We're still growing. When He looks inside us, it's like when He looks at an acorn and sees an oak tree. When He looks at me, He is pleased not because I got it all right today but because He knows what I'm growing into. I'm growing into my Father because the blood of Jesus made a way for that to happen. That acorn, His acorn, is in us.

We are growing into the unity of the faith and of the knowledge of the Son of God to maturity, to the measure of the stature of the fullness of Christ so that we may no longer be children, tossed about by the waves and carried about by every wind of doctrine, by human cunning, by craftiness in deceitful schemes (Ephesians 4:13–14).

Lord, thank You for Your design and timing.
Thank You for who I am in You because of You.
Thank you that because of Your gift of love,
no matter the battle, no matter the circumstances,
I am redeemed.

ACKNOWLEDGMENTS

A giant thank-you to all the people mentioned in this book who have been a huge part of my life. An equally giant thank-you goes to the people not mentioned who played just as large of a role. Even though your name does not appear on a page, you are not forgotten in my heart. Thank you for your investment in my life. Jim, thank you for walking with me through so much of this story. This book never would have been possible without you.

—Mike Weaver

Thank you to all my family and friends who have generously given me their love, encouragement, and support, especially my wife and best friend, Teresa, and my children, Aaron, Joshua, and Jessica; my parents, Richard and Dorothy; my sisters, Diane and Linda, and their families; and to all in the Big Daddy Weave and Whizbang families. Mike, your friendship is one of the great privileges of my life. Thank you for inviting me to walk with you on this journey.

—Jim Scherer

ABOUT THE AUTHORS

MIKE WEAVER is a founding member and the lead singer of Big Daddy Weave, one of Christian music's most beloved artists. The band's numerous number one radio singles are the favorites of many, including "Love Come to Life," "Redeemed," "The Only Name (Yours Will Be)," "Overwhelmed," "My Story," "The Lion and the Lamb," and "Alive." Big Daddy Weave has released multiple full-length albums, received numerous honors, and is widely known for its one-of-a-kind concert performances. Mike and his family live in Mt. Juliet, Tennessee.

www.BigDaddyWeave.com

Instagram & Twitter: @BDWMusic

Facebook: @BigDaddyWeave

JIM SCHERER worked as a creative executive at some of music's most successful companies before founding Whizbang, Inc. Jim's company guides the careers of music artists and facilitates the integration of music in the film, television, video game, and advertising industries. He has managed Big Daddy Weave since 2001. Jim and his family live in Nashville, Tennessee.

www.whizbanginc.com

For more resources and information related to this book, visit
www.iamredeemedbook.com

WHEN THE LIGHT COMES

THE NEW ALBUM FROM BIG DADDY Weave

VISIT **WWW.BIGDADDYWEAVE.COM**
FOR THE LATEST NEWS, CONCERT INFORMATION,
WEBSTORE AND MORE!